CREATIVE COURAGE

By Alex Raffi

DEDICATION

This book is dedicated to the creative child in all of us and to the people who always help me discover mine. To my inspiration: my wife, Debi, and my daughter, Elli. To my mom, dad, and sister. To my teachers and friends and coworkers. And to you, the reader. I hope you are encouraged to reach beyond that red velvet curtain as often as possible.

The wind pressed on a smile.

We gather our intentions and wait.

Our ticking life tips us off to the waiting calm of our discoveries.

Simmering.

It's the noticing that escapes us.

There is a silent scream of invention in our ear.

We are surrounded by it in its silken blackness.

Slightly waving in the breeze.

Light peeks between the drapes.

Now... Now... Now...

We feel that soft slow flash of knowing.

There and gone again.

But it's always there, waiting.

We stretch and reach for it from our seats.

We fail and learn and live with the courage of knowing.

And that is enough,

for now.

CONTENTS

PROLOGUE:
WHY IS CREATIVITY IMPORTANT?

When I was very young, I spent hours reading comic books, sitting in front of the TV, or listening to music. I always had a pencil and paper nearby on which I would draw myriad storyboards of epic adventures that seemed to effortlessly stream from my imagination. Those drawings seemed like treasure maps, each one following a dotted line to another small discovery, another little treasure. If I still had them, they would be a record of the growth of my creative process.

I spent a lot of time in my own head in those days — I still do now but not as much as back then. I remember the hunger for information more than anything. Family members said I didn't talk much as a child, that I just watched everything going on around me, taking it all in. Quiet and curious.

Sometimes, I wish I could go back and imagine the world with the idealism and hope I did in my youth. Without the learned cynicism, doubt, and mistrust. Everything was a door waiting to be opened. Actually, back then I imagined most of the doors were half open, if not wide open, with giant welcome mats. But as I've grown older, those doors have been harder to find, and even when I do find them they are closed.

Children are masters of creativity. There is a purity in a child's creative process because the data is pure. They focus only on need and the data they can access. They are not burdened by fear of judgment. As we get older, we tend to draw from the impressions and expectations of others. We learn to stifle our creativity out of that fear.

When I was a child, I would find a way to incorporate art into any and every situation. Every movie I watched became the focus of my creative endeavors for months. I never stopped exploring my creativity. I'm lucky to have had parents who encouraged me in that exploration. After working in retail, I decided to pursue the arts and become a cartoonist. A local university and newspaper hired me and I was actually paid for my artwork on a regular basis, sheltered from the general perception of how little importance or relevance creativity play in our everyday lives.

Many regard the pursuit of creativity as a waste of time or something available only to the creative "elite." It's poignant but pointless. Yet we are fascinated by the art and entertainment we surround ourselves with. Society admires actors and musicians who have reached creative heights to which we can never aspire, discouraging us from exploring our own creative potential. Have you ever told yourself, "I'll never be that good, so why try?"

We share inspirational poetic verses but tend to live without looking inward or realizing that we must also contribute. Our own creative aspirations are systematically intimidated or stifled. We become impatient and unwilling to take the time required to master a creative craft, instead, living vicariously through the consumption of the creative accomplishments of others. There's a feeling that since we were not born with this inherent ability, learning it would be impossible.

If the extent of our athleticism has been to watch it on television while shoveling chips and soda into our mouths, we're probably not likely to agree to an invitation to run a 5k. The same applies to our creativity. A negative perception of creativity, or a lack of interest in it, is not conducive to creative growth. Such an approach pushes back on a natural need. When we stifle our own creative process, we unwittingly encourage more misunderstandings and support shortsighted solutions. We devolve creatively.

Creativity is not an act or an action; it's an awareness that is actively used in our lives at every moment. We apply it to every action in every manifestation of every thought. Once we begin to think in these terms we can begin to grow and expand our creative potential and improve our creative quotient. We need to reverse the demotivating perception that creativity is something we turn on and off and stand up to our fear of creative inadequacy and failure.

It's interesting how all-encompassing creativity is in our lives, yet we seem to spend so much time squelching its potential. It's time to stop sitting in the audience and begin participating in the play. It's time to push the boundaries of our capacity.

It's why we are here, after all.

1

IF YOU HAVE A PULSE, YOU HAVE A PURPOSE

Descartes takes his date, Jeanne, to a posh restaurant for her birthday. The waiter hands them the wine list, and Jeanne asks to order the most expensive bottle on the list. "I think not!" exclaims an indignant Descartes, and *POOF* he disappears.

"What is the meaning of life?"

Many people spend a lot of time searching for the answer to that question. Is it possible that the answer lies in the question itself?

Our ability to reach far within our own minds and ask a question that big is telling... in many ways. Our need to know the answer can be seen as our purpose. Our need to answer every question in our lives can possibly be the only force that drives us. We are involved at many levels, whether we know it or not, in the progression of our world. Every life is a small part of a bigger organism and our participation, however small, is relevant and part of the endless tapestry of life.

It's important to realize that the fact we have a pulse is the only proof necessary to understand that we have a purpose. And our creativity is the tool we use to exercise that purpose. I believe the terms "creativity" and "problem solving" are interchangeable.

When we open a puzzle box and empty it out onto the table, we are looking at a problem to solve. It is easy to create this problem. Simply overturn the box. The pieces scatter across the table in every direction, at all angles, many landing upside down. Yet every piece has its place. We know this because we can see the solution in the image on the cover of the box. We realize it will take time to find matching pieces and strategically place them near each other. We are not discouraged, because we are sure there is a solution. Every piece has its place.

The world is full of problems, very complicated ones that require the same degree of undiscouraged determination. Manmade problems caused without consideration of consequence. Unfortunately, in everyday life, we don't have the advantage of knowing what the solution looks like. There is no art on the puzzle box. But we do have the ability within us to find it. Once we get to work, the solution will begin to reveal itself.

We also have much smaller problems, run-of-the-mill problems that need to be solved at home or work. We are in a constant state of problem solving. There is virtually no moment in our waking lives where we are not taking note of any given situation, evaluating it and forming an opinion as to how to react or not react. It's important to be aware of these moments and realize that our lack of creative capacity, or in terms of this idea, our lack of being good problem solvers does not come from a lack of experience. It comes from a lack of will. Or rather, it comes from a fear of failure.

We all have the potential to become better problem solvers. It starts with understanding the power and potential of our creativity and having the courage to follow it.

We have been living for a long time with a kind of creative apathy. We take our amazing ability to see, evaluate, react, and execute solutions for granted. If a turning point is encouraged in our perception of creativity, and enough of us champion the cause and become better problem solvers at work, life, and love, then maybe there can be a paradigm shift in the way we react to global problems. This can generate a shift needed to build a better world for our children and our children's children.

In the prologue of *Henry V*, Shakespeare poetically asks his audience to suspend their belief for a moment. He is about to tell an epic story set in fifteenth century England of a young king who lays claim to certain areas of France. This leads to a war between two great kingdoms. He laments about how the humble makings of a small wooden stage, a handful of actors, and stagehands could produce such a massive story.

Aside from some very creative artistry, you can imagine that "special effects" were very limited in the 1600s. Shakespeare struggled with this obstacle. How could he start his play with his audience primed for the story? How could he avoid the initial uphill battle of believability? He came to the conclusion that he would simply ask a favor.

He asks... *"Think when we talk of horses, that you see them printing their proud hoofs i' the receiving earth; For 'tis your thoughts that now must deck our kings, carry them here and there; jumping o'er times, turning the accomplishment of many years into an hour-glass..."*

Shakespeare humbly requested that we delve deeper into our imagination. Not to let ourselves be stifled or limit ourselves to accepted norms or let perceived reality stand in the way of our vision. Shakespeare was challenging the internal skeptic within us, encouraging us to allow ourselves to see with our minds' eyes a scope of possibility beyond the meager visage of what was before us. He asked this because he knew people allowed themselves to be stifled and distracted from seeing possibility.

Understanding creativity requires an acceptance of possibility. We each have perceptions of our own creative capacity, judging our potential on what we have done so far and the results of those past efforts.

I would like to take a note from Shakespeare and call for a muse of fire that might inspire us not to judge creativity on the results of its process. Instead, take note of the capacity of the process undiscovered.

2

MOMENTS OF DISCOVERY

It happens every time we sit to watch a play onstage or see a movie in a theater. As we sit quietly in our seats, we learn and predict the outcomes of every challenge, make assumptions about the plot, and become vested in the show's emotional highs and lows. We live for the pivotal moments presented by the performance. We experience the surprise and adulation for the selfless acts of the heroes, and feel frustration and anger for the injustices doled out by the villains. The world being revealed to us becomes real in our minds' eyes. And if it is done well enough, we can literally feel our hearts sink or swell during the process.

We take voyages to faraway places while we sit comfortably in the dark theater of our perception. We have this amazing ability to imagine things beyond our physical reach and experience them honestly as though they're really happening.

During the creative process, we discover moments and follow ideas within our minds in very much the same way that we do during a show.

We experience a lifetime of emotions and evaluate hundreds of potential outcomes. We balance consequences and weigh options. We do this constantly. Endless scenarios play out in our minds at almost every moment of our lives. We explore, discover, act, and react within this humble stage between our ears. Our mind thrives for the challenge of a goal worthy of it. It's hungry for the struggle because it was made for the struggle.

Our minds need to find solutions, whether we are trying to figure out why there is more matter than antimatter in the observable universe, or deciding what to eat for breakfast. Creativity is our never-ending continuous act of processing information that results in some kind of action or reaction. It allows us to cope with the unexpected and encourages us to reach for new and better solutions. The key is to allow it to do its job, which at times requires courage.

In creativity, the verb is more important than the noun. We are all creative, so the notion that we are creative isn't significant. It is the act of creating that is important, and awareness of this act is key. We need to experience ourselves in the creative process. We need to recognize that we create because we must. We solve problems because there is no alternative. Every choice we make is based on a process of discovery, evaluation, and risk. We need to open up ourselves to realizing that creativity is key to our development and understanding of the world around us. It is our process of learning.

Everyone has a moment of discovery, a moment when our perception widens and we realize something that before was unclear to us. Creativity is fueled by a hunger for those moments. It a process fueled by our natural love of discovery.

So why would creativity require courage? There is a fear that comes with exploration. What a man walking on the tight rope fears is obvious. One miscalculation and he falls to his death. He's reminded of this fear continuously during the walk across that rope.

During the creative process, the fear isn't as clear and present, but the void below us exists just the same. There is no guarantee of success; on the contrary, we find that we often slip. It is much easier to realize what could go wrong than it is to trust our footing. But in much the same way a tightrope walker must face his fears and continue, we must realize that we each possess a net as well. A net woven from every failure and mistake we've made. A net that gets fuller and stronger with every walk. A net made of wit and wisdom.

If we think of our creativity as problem solving, then we can see that we use it endlessly. Every choice or consideration is taken into account. Creativity is not so much an act as it is a habit.

At one of my workshops someone once asked: "How do you know when it's okay to turn off your creativity so that you can actually get some work done?" My response was simple. "When you are done smelling freshly baked bread, do you remove your nose and place it in your pocket?"

Creativity works the same way. We don't turn it on or off. We don't roam the earth carrying our noses in our pockets until we spot a flower and decide to pull them out, attach delicately under our eyes, and then bend down to enjoy the fragrance and then return our noses to our pockets.

Consider for a moment all the smells we would have missed if this were true. We couldn't consciously predict every moment we would have benefitted from an unexpected need to smell something.

Creativity is attached to us. There is a false belief that for us to be creative, we need to be aware of the act or prepare ourselves for the execution of a creative journey. In reality, we have never and will never reach the end of the journey.

Creativity is not a tactic; it's biological and ever present, endlessly working. Our ability to improve on it requires an understanding of this idea.

3
AWARENESS

I remember playing in the dirt as a child and suddenly having a deep moment of clarity. Something triggered it — maybe the warmth of the sun on the back of my neck as it peeked through a cloud — and it woke me up. Suddenly I could hear the silence. I took pause for a moment and began taking inventory of the time. To this day I can remember that feeling. I can see and smell the moist black earth on my hands, hear the birds in the trees, and feel the slight sting on my scratched-up knees in the damp grass. I took notice of the fact that I was young and loved by my parents and little sister. I allowed myself to be curious about my future, and wondered if I would still want to dig in the dirt when I grew up. I was alone but not lonely. In some strange way I was in tune with my awareness.

You can do this right now, no matter where you are. Use all of your senses to capture this moment and encapsulate it in your memory. Make a mental note of what is happening right now. Consider what you are hearing, smelling, or feeling on your skin. Take it all in — and let that take you to the next level of perception. Follow your intuition. It doesn't need to be a revelation. The act itself becomes a simple revelation that will prove to be valuable at some point in your life. Take a moment now to put this book down and make yourself aware of what is happening around you. Stop reading, put the book down, and *be still...*

...

...

...

...

We tend to ignore intimacy with our own lives. There is real value in simply paying attention. The act of pausing our distractions and considering the moments provides opportunities to see things we may have missed that can lead us into new discoveries. We often ignore moments that are filled with learning opportunities, but when we pause, we cast a net into our lives that has the potential to capture a new idea or realization; we create a chance to learn something.

But teaching and learning doesn't only happen in a classroom or even between people. Sometimes, just being aware is enough. We miss countless learning opportunities in our everyday lives by not paying attention. We often overlook the fact that we are our own best teachers. We learn what we want to learn at any given time. Knowledge is a suggestion. We decide its value.

Here is an uncomfortable question for some. How many times have we taken the time to revel in our own genius? Though we have used a lifetime of deductive reasoning to solve a major problem, we often don't give ourselves the credit we deserve. We forget to give ourselves credit for those times we perform at our best when reasoning and problem solving. Living within our moments is very important and it's easy to take our own greatness for granted. It's natural to be humble, but the truth is we are all amazing. Even the simplest exercise in deductive reasoning has the potential to become a breakthrough that can change your life.

Think back to a time when you evaluated your options and came up with a solution that surprised you and those around you. At that moment, you had an opportunity to learn something through a conscious awareness of your action. If you realize that your process of discovery and development isn't an accident and that you can actively participate in its development by merely acknowledging its existence, you might come up with these surprising solutions more often and more quickly.

One way to create a moment is to strike up a conversation with a stranger. If I'm waiting in line or sitting in a place within talking distance, I'll try to find a reason to interact with another person. When was the last time someone you didn't know showed true interest in you and your ideas without an agenda? People tend to dig deeply when this happens. It's a gift of chance for them, and if you're lucky, many times this gift leads to a fascinating discussion filled with life lessons and interesting revelations. In a world filled with narcissistic distractions, it's sometimes difficult to make time for other perceptions' influence and be inspired by a life foreign to your own. Every question you have acts as bait for potentially powerful data that can be used to decode a life mystery. Gathering qualified data is important to the quality of our creative resolutions.

We create opportunities to be inspired when we pay attention to our own actions, but the feeling of inspiration we get is not given to us. We make a choice. We decide what is inspiring. Learning to inspire ourselves can become addicting. We begin to seek out possibilities and start exploring new ideas that at one time may have discouraged us. Anything we can do to stimulate our natural need of inspiration is valuable. Take every opportunity that comes our way, but more importantly, create those opportunities and always remember to experience ourselves in those moments.

It may not always seem like it, but we all have managed to figure out how to use the most complicated technology in the known universe: the human mind. It is the only tool we have that truly matters. It controls our perception, memory, abstract thought, complex behavior, and consciousness. We still don't understand it, but understanding it isn't necessarily critical to using it, just as we don't need to know everything about how a violin works to master it.

According to neuropsychologist Rick Hanson, Ph.D., our mind is capable of amazing things...

"On average, each of the 100 billion neurons in your head has about 1000 connections with other neurons, creating a huge network of about 100 trillion synapses. Like a computer network built from one hundred trillion transistors, each representing a "bit" of information depending on whether it is "on" or "off."

Adding up all possible combinations of 100 billion neurons firing or not, the number of potential states of that neuronal network is approximately 10 to the millionth power: one followed by a million zeros."

(*Your Wonderful Brain*

http://www.rickhanson.net/wonderful-brain/)

Think of that the next time you allow these "bits" to manifest themselves into the notion that you can't do something. Ignore the negative message and get back to work. I'm pretty sure your brain can handle it.

Picture a small bird wearing a top hat. The bird is purple with yellow stripes, playing a piano. Within a split second of reading this description, you've been able to imagine exactly what I described. Yet you have never seen a creature like that before. We can create entire worlds in our imagination. It's a very powerful tool.

The complexity of our intellectual capacity is evident when we dream. While asleep, we experience stories and perceive them as real. It's as though we are watching a movie playing out before us and we are part of that story. We are the actors, directors, set designers, producers, etc. We play every part, yet at the same time, we are the audience, experiencing every moment as if it's the first time we have ever seen it. We are startled by the sudden turn of events in the very nightmare we've authored.

How is this possible? How are we capable of creating ideas that inspire us to consider other ideas? We have a dualism in our creative perception that allows us to manifest ideas beyond our expectations, yet we treat our creativity as a novelty. It is true that we are influenced and react to ideas presented to us, but are we influenced by or reacting only to a selected few of them? Are we auditing potential? If so, why? And are our reasons for being selective valid?

During our lifetimes, we gather data and discover our own perceptions. When we become aware of our perceptions, it's almost as if we're learning about them from another source. We are, in essence, leading ourselves into other discoveries and opportunities. Our conscious minds have an amazing capacity to realize possibility, but we tend only to scratch the surface. We are capable, through sheer will, to create and discover many potential outcomes simultaneously.

The world is your backyard. Take time to realize those moments when you dig into your own intellectual dirt.

Think about an act of problem solving or an exchange of ideas with colleagues. Consider that entire moment now, and think about what motivated each act among the people involved. What was the motivation to find the solution? Was it finding the solution, or feeling the need to be the problem solver? Was everyone being open minded to each others' ideas? Did you all encourage each other? Did you allow yourself to have your mind changed?

Don't consider the result, consider the process that led up to the result. Were you acting as an instigator in a positive way or a negative way? Were you being the architect of the moment, or were you just along for the ride? Or were you reacting to the random developments as they came forward?

Have you ever actively pushed an idea into a moment that changed the outcome? If you have, it likely caused a shift of some sort in everyone's thinking.

If we take time to consider our moments, these questions are easily answered. We are more aware of who we are and how we do things. In turn, we become hyper–aware of who our colleagues and friends are, and we understand them better. We collect valuable information necessary to move ideas forward. We begin to understand how to encourage and inspire people to pitch in and deliver necessary direction for better solutions. This provides us with the courage to explore possibilities more confidently.

It's good to dive into the ocean for the sake of the experience. Although it can be dangerous, it may also be enlightening. I had an experience in Maui that is a great example of this concept. Although my experience could have resulted in a termination of my moments, instead, it evoked a powerful memory. I chose to consider it as a lesson as opposed to a mistake. It now has value for me.

It's an awakening I can use to build on who I am and why I do what I do.

In July of 2012 my family and I went to the Hawaiian Islands. I learned quite a bit about myself on that trip. The power of stillness that I first experienced as a child was strong there. I caught myself noticing my moments, experiencing myself in the act of noticing. Reflecting on the ***now*** in a way that was reminiscent of the way I had as a child. I would try and capture that particular moment in my memory as much as possible. *"I AM, Now"* I would think to myself. I hadn't felt that realization for a long time. The clarity of those moments held tight enough to my memories that I was able to recall them quite clearly.

So I sat in a wooden chair in a balcony and really looked at the landscape before me and then drew my attention in to the peeled tangerine on my armrest. There was a beauty in the uniqueness to the texture that I could relate to the moment. I actively searched for those escapes into these "Now" moments. Sending my attention outward like a fishing net and then pulling the net back, gathering what I saw and examining it, created an intimacy with my surroundings. Now whenever I see or peel a tangerine, it takes me back to that beautiful green landscape and waterfall.

Inspiration is everywhere. But it still requires us to make an effort. There is a line in the Tom Waits song, "New Coat of Paint" that says, *"Love needs a transfusion, let's shoot it full of wine/ Fishing for a good time starts with throwing in your line."* It's important to actively experience our moments and our engagement with the moments because they create definable memories that can be used as the basis for idea building. It reminds us of what we value, and creates opportunity for innovation and creativity.

One afternoon, while at a hotel on the island of Maui, I left my wife and daughter at the pool and went, unbeknownst to them, for a walk on the beach. I stepped into the perfect water and there it was again. Deciding to explore a bit farther, I rented some snorkeling gear and headed into the ocean. I awkwardly put on the mask and flippers and swam out. As I sunk my head into the water, the sudden silencing of the yelling, splashing tourists surrounding me felt like a massive door had shut behind me. The amazing scene of colorful fish and coral before me made the world above me seem like it was in black and white. It was, in a word, magic. I slowly swam and took in the sights, doing my best to survey everything around me. An impossibly white school of fish swam past me. I followed it as far as I could, truly lost in the experience.

After a while I realized I was getting tired. I wasn't an avid swimmer and was clearly not in as good a shape as I may have thought. I popped my head up to start heading back and discovered that I had swum very far from shore — very, very far. I was, in fact, farther from shore than anyone within sight. I realized I had no other option than to put my head down and swim back with the little energy I had left. So I took a deep breath and swam hard toward the shore. After a while I lifted my head, hoping I was close enough to possibly touch the ground with my foot and was shocked to see I had not moved any closer to the shore.

Looking back on that moment, I'm surprised to say, I didn't panic. I got mad. I got mad at myself for allowing this to happen. For allowing myself to get into a situation I couldn't control. But as tired as I was, I had no other option than to keep swimming. For some reason, I removed my mask and snorkel and swam as hard as I could for as long as I could.

Eventually, I saw a woman on a surfboard and called out to her with a feeble wave. She responded by waving back with a smile and paddling away. This made me even angrier than before. The best I could muster was a pathetic dog paddle, taking shallow breaths and counting every stroke. I felt my muscles cramping up but now was close enough to call out to a person playing along the shore, who leapt into the water like some kind of aquatic superhero. I remember this heroic man grabbing my arm and yelling, "Swim!" "Swim!" and me thinking to myself that he seemed a tad overdramatic, but I really appreciated the help and enthusiasm. I thanked him, and once I was able to touch the ground I slowly walked myself to shore and collapsed.

I lay down on the sand feeling angry and ashamed. It was then that I had one of my biggest moments of clarity. I realized that I had almost jeopardized my life and the future of my wife and daughter. They had no idea I even went into the ocean. I had another *"I AM, Now"* moment that felt very different from any other. I had escaped tragedy by the skin of my teeth. But I kept swimming. I never even considered the idea of giving up.

This was another of many problems I was meant to solve, like everything I'd identified and acknowledged in the past. All my past solutions to seemingly unsolvable problems intersected when I realized that I'd better get back to shore before it was too late. I really believe it was my want to solve a problem that got me back, not my will to survive. I became intensely focused and driven to get back.

I pushed my wall further down the road. My "Now" moments are not there for my amusement. They are reminders of my capacity. I need to make the most of them. Those moments I spent fighting the currents of the North Pacific taught me the idea that life is lived in seconds and minutes, all heading in one direction. There is nothing before me other than a string of "Now" moments, each leading to the next. I am grateful I had the wherewithal to keep going that day. And although my situation was dire, I saw it as a problem to solve and a moment that was meant to lead me to the next moment. I think of this a lot now.

We are a collection of our moments. Our interpretation of those moments is very valuable in shaping the way we view the world. It dictates how we react or approach any given situation. Learning from our moments takes a willingness to see the lessons within them. Interpretation of a collection of actions, assessing the reactions to those actions and then seeing the result within the scope of a bigger meaning opens us up to another, deeper perception that we may have missed otherwise.

4

THE WILD GARDEN OF OUR CHILDHOOD

Everything is ceremony in the wild garden of childhood.
— Pablo Neruda

We get comfortable in our mediocrity when we grow old. We lose that wide-eyed wonder that molded us. We internalize life. A child, on the other hand, thrives in life. Children are an open nerve, feeling life. The way we processed our perception of the world around us when we were young was powerful and deep. We grow older and learn how to be afraid. We replace our wonder and curiosity with a need to imitate and emulate. The reward we received to keep that sense of wonder was never made clear to us as children because everyone around us encouraged us to leave it behind as they did. Our want for clear tangible results pushed out the obvious need for the process required to get them. We became content with the echoing of perceptions of those around us. We lost our patience for the discovery. We neglected the child within us patiently waiting for us to ask for guidance.

There is power in that simplicity. We mistake childish perception as naive or simplistic. On the contrary, there is a deep purity to childish perception. We must begin to identify that perception as qualified creative courage.

Have you ever looked at a child's drawing of a person? Many drawings I've seen have been a rudimentary circle with two dots for eyes and a big smiley mouth with arms and legs coming off the circle. A bit like this:

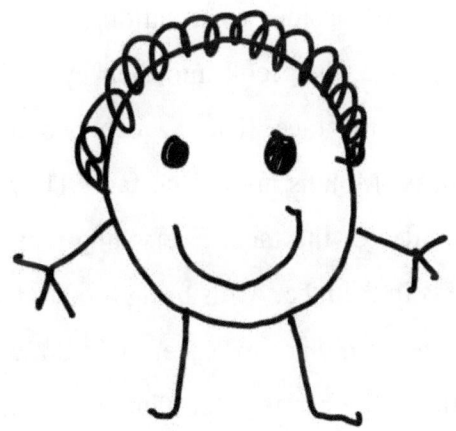

Many might find this drawing charming or cute, but I'm more curious of our opinion of the process. Consider how we tend to judge artwork or the ideas of others. Do we set expectations based on the content or on our initial expectations of the content? Do we apply that consideration to this drawing, for example, or do we consider the source and the goal of the one who expressed this idea? We may believe that this drawing is not a good representation of what a person looks like, and we might conclude that it's lack of sophistication is because it was drawn by a child. But if we consider that the child's intent was not to impress our notions of what his or her art should look like, we may begin to see this drawing differently.

Take a moment to consider what children see. When they interact with people, they look into their eyes, don't they? The eyes are on the face. They watch people's mouths when they speak. Mouths are on the face. They hear from ears on both sides of the face. Everything they know and see of people is in the face. Arms bring food to the face and legs get the face from place to place. Their drawings depict their perception of what is important in a person. From their perspective, it's the moments of engagement and tools used in those engagements that defines a person, not the torso.

This is what is missing from our perception as we grow older and limit ourselves creatively. We begin to have a need to impress others by communicating ideas in an excepted format. But that limits us. We edit ourselves out of reaching our creative need to find the wonderful of things. The richness of things we feel we can't express in an exceptional way.

How many of us have had something wonderful to share and not had the words to express it? Is it a lack of words or the notion that others may not understand our idea? That lack of articulation may come from a need to satisfy what we believe others may think. We spend a lot of time editing our own ideas down to mediocrity for the sake of what... clarity?

Give others the benefit of the doubt. Challenge them to meet us where we live creatively. Invite them in. They may get confused; then again, they may get inspired. Either way, it's worth a chance. Because if it goes well and people begin to see the deeper meaning in their own way of thinking through our honest expression, then we are really standing shoulder to shoulder with our creative capacity.

We need to strive to see the world through younger eyes. We need to live with the fearless sense of expression of a child. Stripping away the binding fear of judgment will clear the path to innovating ways of seeing our creative potential.

5

KAKORRHAPHIOPHOBIA

Creative Courage *with Alex Raffi*

Kakorrhaphiophobia:
The abnormal fear of failure or defeat

The way we respond to failures, criticisms, or inconveniences will likely reflect how we will react to a creative opportunity as it presents itself. Not all opportunities seem initially valuable. The majority require the effort of being placed into context, analyzed and remembered.

Our overreaction to a negative notion can kill our progress toward developing a solution. Our frustration with our own ability not to have the answer now feeds our failure. Our perceptions set the tone for the outcome of everything we do. If we believe creativity is a skillset that we are gifted at birth, then we will likely justify our own limitations and never try to grow creatively. We see the remarkable achievements of others and decide we can never exceed or even match that achievement. We say to ourselves, "What is the point of trying?" and at times, strive for mediocrity. It's much easier to settle into our limitations. It's safer to avoid failure so we are not reminded of our unfortunate lack of creative capacity.

I realized that within the context of my artwork people perceived my creative ability as 'special.' "I wish I could draw like you," was something I heard constantly. It made me feel good and motivated me to continue but also made me wonder if I was different in some way. But what was different about me? By some accounts I was pretty average; by others, below average. But I could draw.

The perception people tend to have about the creative process is that only some of us have somehow been able to create slightly higher than mediocre artwork. It seems obvious to everyone that some of us are just good at creating interesting and innovative ideas from thin air. That creativity is an ability we are able to carry around with us. As if it sits nestled in our pockets waiting to be pulled out and used. Creative people are seen as quirky and eccentric. Their power, although seemingly elusive and unique, is considered quaint and distracting. Valued as a genetic bonus. Not considered a key to anything but entertainment.

It's a common misconception that creative capacity is predestined. The idea that some of us are born with better creative perception comes from the idea that creativity is a skill, like juggling or origami. But is this true? Can only some of us have the ability to dig deeper into our creative talents and execute innovative and amazing solutions?

The truth is, the only thing that advances a well-tuned sense of creativity is a *want*. An improved creative capacity is not an unreachable goal that requires endless research and development. It comes simply from a want. We need a want to be open to more things. We need a want to explore areas that we may not consider valuable. We need a want to feel failure and disappointment because it teaches us how to avoid failure and disappointment more effectively. We need to stop making assumptions on what being creative means or comparing our capacity to those of others. Wanting to open up to new ideas and notions of innovation is a powerful thing. A journey we must take on our own.

It is also possible that we have failed to identify our creative capacity. We may not see our ability to solve math problems as a part of our creative process. But as we are doing a math problem, don't we need to use the same tools within us that the world's greatest artists have used to express their ideas? We look at possibilities and deduce a plan of action from those possibilities. We react to learned strategies that have proven to be effective, but when faced with a problem we've never seen before, we immediately begin a journey of possibility. We weigh risks and execute ideas we have judged valuable. That's what we do, all the time, every waking moment of our lives. We solve problems.

6

PEEKING THROUGH THE CURTAIN

How often do you ask yourself the question, "Who am I?" Are you sure you know? Do you know what inspires you? If I asked you that question, would you pause and have to think about the answer? If so, it's not at the top of your mind, is it?

Ask yourself that question and write your initial answer here:

_____**inspires me.**

By the end of this book it will be interesting to come back and see if this is still your answer.

Many things limit our process of creative exploration. It's different for each of us. Taking time to examine your own creative process should reveal some of them. Auditing the difficulty of the process or trying to guess the outcome and basing your strategy on that assumption limits what you explore when considering your belief of what you can accomplish.

Picture a long red velvet curtain surrounding you. Imagine it about twenty feet away from you in all directions. Wherever you go it follows.

This curtain represents our perceived limit to our creative capacity. We only see opportunism that is visible within the circle of red. Everything we understand and are comfortable with sits inside this curtain. We can see every opportunity easily and reach it with little to no effort. And after a while we believe that is all there is. Our world of possibility lies within this circle of curtain.

But every once in a while we get a glimpse of what's on the other side. Sometimes we can see a little light peeking between the drapes. A flash of brilliance maybe. We notice it periodically, but most of the time, it's ignored because it's unfamiliar or irrelevant.

Those small flashes from the other side of the curtain are hints of our creative capacity. It's our subconscious mind tossing us a line, hoping we will grab it and bring it into our realm of awareness.

We are governed creatively by the limits of our risk tolerance. It protects us from danger but also keeps us from taking chances on anything new or foreign. We set our own creative bar based on what we've seen others accomplish. We don't consider, or even realize, that most people who have succeeded or excelled in their creative ability have done so after multiple failures. A simple search on the web will reveal many quotes from notable creatives that document this idea.

> *Only those who dare to fail greatly*
> *can ever achieve greatly.*
> — Robert Kennedy

It's easy to forget how much there is to be excited about in every new discovery. There is fluidity with ideas. They pour out like water, sometimes breaking apart and inspiring new ideas. It's important to slow down and allow the process to move forward. Enjoy the process. The time we spend will be valuable to becoming more aware and more efficient in that awareness. Time is a powerful friend to the creative process. Wasted time is a terrible thing. But time doing what we love or what makes us better is never wasted. It's about how we perceive the time spent on the process. Do we see it as pointless? Or do we see it as a valuable part of our individual creative evolution?

We are an accumulation of our experiences. We capture information from whatever moment we are in and hold it close. The sum of those moments becomes our perception of everything in our lives. The only thing we have to temper and shape that information is the way the world reacts to us as we engage it. The responses we get from those engagements, whether good or bad, become comfortable and safe, because we hold them as truths based on our experience with them, not necessarily because we believe in our potential.

To borrow another metaphor from Neruda's poem, we are always "casting our nets," hoping to capture wisdom. We try to unlock the world's mysteries, but at the end of the day we discover that the answers we capture in that net are our own learned beliefs based on our fears and loves, victories and failures. All molded from the life we are living. We judge the answers, keeping only the acceptable parts that are comfortable to our existence. We decide how far we can go. We make the choices that build and bind us. It's important to remember we are never done learning or growing intellectually.

Ask yourself if you are willing to work for a better purpose or if you are willing to settle.

7
DATA

Many years ago my wife and I were driving into the city of Cork in the Republic of Ireland. We were looking for a hotel near a little pub called the Crows Nest and wanted to get something to eat before turning in. On the way I noticed a woman walking along the sidewalk by the road. I pulled up near her and asked if she knew the way to the pub. She paused and thought sincerely for a moment. She gestured in one direction, then corrected herself and stared down in thought. At this point it began to rain. She took out an umbrella and continued thinking.

I said, "No worries! Thanks anyway, we'll find it!" and began to drive away. I wasn't going to have that woman stand in the rain struggling to give me directions. But as I pulled away, she called out, "Wait! I know where it is."

I continued pulling away, assuring her that it was fine and not to worry, but she chased us alongside yelling out directions. And although I kept yelling to her, "It's okay! Thank you! We'll find it! Stop running!" she was determined to help a car full of American strangers get to their destination.

I remember that story every time someone I don't know asks me for a favor. I make it an important moment. It's a shift in my normal existence. It's a chance to connect unexpectedly with someone and utilize my ability to adapt in some way. I didn't see much shyness from people in Ireland. Everyone seemed to have time for each other.

I believe those moments are valuable when considering how we gather data from each other. If we begin to see experiences as valuable resources for data in our lives, we may be more open to exploring them more frequently and more generously. Opportunities surround us at every moment. We don't always see them, but they are there if we take the time to notice them.

The rain that came down on my Irish friend is a good metaphor for how data rains down on us throughout our lives. For the moment, imagine that a raindrop represents a portion of data. One drop might represent a horse and another a bird. Now we combine those drops and create a Pegasus.

Picture yourself standing in the rain. Have you ever stood in the rain and looked up? The falling drops fan out, surrounding you as they fall. The drops are endless, always falling, impossible to count. We capture what we can and let the rest disappear with a splash. Some of the drops slip by us. But there is no reason to get discouraged. More is always falling within your reach. We make a choice to either drop the umbrella and allow the rain to wash over us or pull our coats tighter and hunker down through the storm.

The act of acceptance or denial of opportunities requires a want. We are given the choices to act or ignore this data during every waking moment. Shifting our attitude through awareness and a willingness to take it all in can allow for many more creative possibilities.

The choice we make can have a massive impact on the outcome of our process. Ideas, perceptions, and feeling every experience is within those drops. Imagine opportunity as a never-ending rain that covers the entire earth. Imagine every raindrop as data that can be used to solve problems, understand language, inspire emotions, or deliver expectations. Every drop holds promise. Now imagine how many of these drops in a lifetime of rain actually touch us. How many have we sheltered ourselves from? How many have we taken and absorbed to create a solution?

We huddle in the warmth of our contentment and understanding of how things seem to be. We unwittingly shield ourselves from information necessary to creatively process manageable solutions, important questions, bigger understandings, and stronger communications, and begin to develop and enhance conscious realization.

Data comes in all forms. It can be a feeling we may want to remember or repeat. It can be a smell that inspires another memory. It can be something said in passing that has stuck with us, a line in a newspaper article, or the smile of a child. Data is what we notice. It's also what we don't even realize we notice. A willingness to notice will become intuition necessary for our unconscious mind to take in those moments we don't realize.

Actively understanding that data is out there for us to take in is a powerful creative perception. We can't predict the value of the data until it is processed and even then its value may never be noticed. But gathering data is as simple as accepting the coolness of a rainstorm. If we are aware of its existence, we are almost there. Pay attention. Listen and see the opportunities around us and consider that our moments are the fuel of our memory and intuition. We are defined by those moments. In essence, we are gathering the materials needed to build these moments. The more data we have the more depth and value our processes will have.

If we remember, the rain is out there, always falling, always present. And if we believe it is our job to make the effort and capture the raindrops, we will begin to clearly see that there are endless opportunities we can gather to build and explore possibility. There is no limit to the rain.

If the rain doesn't seem to fall on us as heavily as we would like — it feels like a drizzle — remember that we are capable of finding bigger storms by exploring new places or ideas. Meet new people. Share our moments and watch others be inspired from the sharing. All that is required is a want to grow. It's up to us to bravely close the umbrella, lay it down, open our arms to the sky, and feel the rain on our faces.

8
BAD DATA

We often give ourselves way too much credit for having the right answer to the wrong questions.

In the hilarious book, *The Hitchhiker's Guide to the Galaxy*, by Douglas Adams, there is a moment when a famous question is posed: "What is the answer to the ultimate question of life, the universe and everything?" Inputting the question into a supercomputer named Deep Thought, the answer provided after a very long wait — 7.5 million years — was "42."

The computer, noticing the confusion its answer caused the people, explained further saying the true problem was that nobody really understood the question. Hence, the reason they also did not understand the answer.

I ask that you indulge my attempt to find the right question to that mysterious answer. I would like to think that if this silly story were true, the real question to the answer of life, the universe, and everything might be this: "How many of these questions can you answer 'yes' to?"

If your answer is "42," then you've already figured out the answer.

1. Are you happy?
2. Do you laugh daily?

3. Does anyone love you?

4. Do you love someone?

5. Are you challenged daily?

6. Are you proud of your work?

7. Are you proud of your choices?

8. Can you trust the people around you?

9. Can you solve problems?

10. Are you contributing to the lives of others?

11. Are you a good person?

12. Are you doing your best?

13. Are you teaching?

14. Are you learning?

15. Are you part of the solution?

16. Do you have empathy?

17. Do you try to make a difference?

18. Do you make time for yourself?

19. Do you hold the door open for others? (Literally and metaphorically.)

20. Do you try to experience other cultures?

21. Do you try to surprise yourself?

22. Do you wonder why things are the way they are?

23. Do you work to live, instead of live to work?

24. Do you do things that are difficult?

25. Do you tell people what you like about them?

26. Do you allow yourself to have your mind changed?

27. Are you able to manage your ego constructively?

28. Are you brave enough to try to understand the pain of others?

29. Have you ever helped a stranger?

30. Have you ever attempted to create something?

31. Have you ever shed tears of pride and joy?

32. Do you appreciate what you have, no matter how little?

33. Have you ever expressed your true self to anyone?

34. Have you ever stood up for someone who needed help?

35. Have you ever forgiven an enemy?

36. Have you ever given help anonymously?

37. Do you ever make time to notice something beautiful?

38. Do you try to improve the lives of those around you?

39. Do you listen?

40. Do you see?

41. Do you lead by example?

42. Do you share what you've learned?

Many times we are given information to work with that has not been adequately considered. We spend hours working really hard finding an answer to a question built on bad data. Bad data happens.

So how do we know if we have the right or wrong data? First start by identifying if we even need a solution.

There are many ways to approach a solution. A very popular way is to amend an old idea to try to make it new again. Applying new twists to old solutions that have proven successful in the past.

Take, for instance, the pencil. It is a great idea. It's an instrument for writing or drawing, consisting of a thin stick of graphite or a similar substance enclosed in a long thin piece of wood. Its simplicity is elegant and its purpose is sure. It is an idea that has impacted our world in unimaginable ways. It has been a key tool used to express ideas, communicate dreams, and calculate the density of solar systems. It has been universally used in homes, governments, businesses, and schools across the globe. It's very likely one is within eyeshot at this very moment.

But let's say that after a while in light of other inventions or innovations the pencil has lost its perceived value. Even cultural and technological trends this great idea seem outdated. So a comity is formed to discuss a plan of how to improve this once amazingly innovative idea. The plan is now to find ways to make this old idea new again. The easiest way to do this is to change the idea by adding an amendment to it, to make the original idea seem fresh. Then another is added and another. But the perception still doesn't change. This failure tends to wrongly be blamed on the original idea. The comity fails to realize it is the amendments that are not working, not the original innovation.

We need to remember when revisiting old "great ideas" to establish what made them great in the first place. Realize its relevant impact. We must build on it and then go forward with a plan that will insert the same innovations in a way that is more relevant to the current changing environment. Great ideas need to evolve from its core up. The tendency is to focus on what we perceive as being negative and try and disguise or hide that, instead of focusing on what was great about the original idea and shining a light on it and building from there.

If we find ourselves on a rescue mission for a once great idea, remember to give the old idea the credit it deserves. If we revisit what made the original idea great in the first place and build on it, taking into consideration our current needs, we may find a solution with longevity and purpose that will prove to be a true rebirth of its former greatness.

In essence, we need to go back as far as we can to see what the real need is. Find the "Why" first. Then "What" and "How." Why do we need this solution? What is the best approach to solving it? And how are we going to begin?

We can't let bad data ruin the results of our process. We must do our best to consider if it is what we need.

9

FALLING UPWARD

There are days I feel like a man in the eye of a tornado. Millions of precious things I need spin violently around me. Ideas, memories, hopes, and opportunities. I reach out to grab them as they roar by. I touch a few. It's never clear what they are until I touch them. They sting the tips of my fingers. Every once in a while the moment is perfect and the approach is clear. What I least expect lands firmly in my hand and I understand. I put it in my pocket. It weighs heavy with other precious things.

We take in our days with the familiarity of comfort. We believe in our predictions. We depend on the consistency of our survival while forsaking exposure to a deeper consideration. We tell ourselves that there is little hope in chance even while we are within the moment of taking chances. But we have all wandered. We have all walked into the dark places with wide eyes and have been elevated by the discovery. Those moments are not chance exploration. Those moments define our "why." They are the essence of what makes us believe in our truth. They are manifestations of our creativity and courage. A new belief holds power. A power that spreads like a raging fire. But this fire builds rather than destroys. Only leaving the charred remains of fear and self-doubt in its path. It inspires us and enlightens us to the possibilities. It shines light on opportunity. We do this. We are the builders of this fire and at times don't realize it. We diminish it because we were not the architects of the inspiration. We stoke the flames and call it luck. We make the conscious choice to explore and discover and don't take credit for the success we reveal.

It's important to know when to speak and when to listen. Learning and teaching take equal shares of courage. Accepting a new idea may feel like standing on the edge of a rocky cliff and letting ourselves fall forward. But it's important to realize that there is no gravity in the creative process. We are in control. We need to allow ourselves to fall upward. Realize that our ideas can become a source of inspiration for someone else. Giving begets getting. A shared idea can inspire a thought that might expand on that idea exponentially and unexpectedly. Learning and teaching, listening and sharing are the most important things we can do for each other.

The essence of creation is an openness to be inspired by ourselves and others. We are all on the same journey of discovery. Some actively explore; others stumble onto what finds them. But the journey is the same. The processing of information and reaction to data is the same as used by a musician, for example, to create a beautiful piece of music. It's all problem solving. It's the thing that allows us to evolve and continue to go forward. It's the clearest reflection of our humanity.

Some of us live as observers of others' creations and define ourselves by our judgment of them. The rest of us create our experience. Piece by piece we expand our capacity to understand and learn. We weave layers upon layers of realization and action together to create our lives. We all have the ability to notice, act, build, and express ourselves.

A big part of understanding our own creative capacity is to realize that society as a whole suffers from a shallowness of perception. We tend to place judgment using only surface data to substantiate our conclusions on how to act. We need to realize we have to go deeper in our process. We need to slow down and think. Thoughtfulness in the creative process is becoming a lost art. Consideration of global perception is important in communication because it keeps our points focused. Awareness of our creative potential is a choice. Whenever we are able to take that extra step toward a deeper understanding of something, we should do so.

Being self-aware during our creative development is fulfilling it. The act of noticing the process also feeds it. There is richness in surprising our selves that is deeply inspiring. By paying attention we can identify areas we may be stifling. Realizing what moves us and how much we keep ourselves from exploring those moments can be very valuable in our creative development, and a necessary first step in harnessing the richness of our creative capacity.

A sparrow flies over a forest in search of a nesting place. Following her natural intuition and cunning, she identifies a possible location to begin building. The sparrow lands and evaluates the area closer from deep within the forest. She considers the safety of her choice. And once her choice is justified, the sparrow springs into action gathering twigs and leaves and begins weaving a nest that becomes a soft and safe resting place for her small and very fragile eggs. But that's just the beginning of the process. With a bit of nurturing and love, within a few weeks, eggs hatch with new birds that will one day do the same.

If we are working on solving a problem or trying to come up with an innovation or notion, it's best to start from way up high.

Look at the issue from a bird's eye view and zero in on your concept. Gather ideas and weave a solution. Once you have a solution in place, there is one more step to take, one that is often forgotten: nurture it and watch it grow on its own. The success of that solution will inspire even more ideas. It's the circle of life AND ideas.

Groundbreaking innovations have one thing in common. They were inspired by a need that led to a creative process unafraid of the possibility of failure.

Before every endeavor a calculation occurs in our minds. Is my next step justified? Is the act of accomplishing this goal beneficial to an immediate or long-term need? And is this worth the effort necessary to accomplish it? If we answer no to any of these question we're likely to move on to something else. But people who have done great things or even little things have all answered a resounding "YES!" to every one of those questions. So the question becomes, how do we choose to limit ourselves. What is our capacity? How much do we trust our ability to resolve those questions?

Our intellectual capacity is hard to define. But we know it is there. It's powerful and mysterious. Understanding what it is and why it's there is less important than just accepting that it is there and we must use it to learn as much as possible. Eventually it may let us in on its secrets. That's the nature of creative exploration. We never know what we might come across.

What was said to the rose that made it open
was said to me here in my chest.
What was told the Cypress that made it strong
and straight, what was
whispered the jasmine so it is what it is, whatever made
sugarcane sweet, whatever
was said to the inhabitants of the town of Chigil in
Turkestan that makes them
so handsome, whatever lets the pomegranate flower blush
like a human face, that is
being said to me now. I blush. Whatever put eloquence in
language, that's happening here.
The great warehouse doors open; I fill with gratitude,
chewing a piece of sugarcane,
in love with the one to whom every that belongs!
*   – Jalaluddin Rumi*

10
THE JOURNEY

When my wife and I first started dating we loved to watch the sunset. Those moments became symbolic in our lives. Whenever something great happened we called it a "sunset moment."

We married in 1996 and have spent every anniversary in the same cottage on a beach in San Diego. In 2003 my daughter began joining us in this traditional getaway. On one of these visits, my daughter and I spent the day playing in the waves and building sandcastles. I noticed the amazing sunset and mentioned it to her.

She looked up and smiled at me as if to say, "I got it, it's the sun. Thanks, Dad."

I tried to explain how amazing it looked and how beautiful the light was reflecting off the wet sand, but it was pointless. She was dragging a piece of seaweed across the sand and drawing Homer Simpson with it. She didn't have time for my sentimental notions.

The next day it came to me that the sunset moment was mine. It wasn't her moment to notice. She, in fact, was my sunset moment. I may as well have been asking the ocean to take notice of the stars. At that moment, she was a big reason I was taking it all in. In time she will develop her own sunset moments to appreciate. It made me realize that we each have our own unique journey to discover.

It's important to think about what is going on in our minds during problem solving. All the choices that are being considered, all the past examples we re-evaluate, and outcomes we consider. Imagine the inventory audit and analysis. All the digressions we manage and deconstruct. All the simulations we review in our minds, considering past advice and experience. This all happens in what seems to be seconds if not less. There is an entire journey we travel when analyzing a problem.

The fact that we aren't able to physically see this journey is unfortunate. If we were able to actually watch it play out above our heads like a floating equation, we would see evidence of how amazing the creative process is. But since we aren't able to watch the process we are left with placing judgment on creativity based on the results. All the credit deserving to the process goes to the result of the process. I believe we need to reverse that idea. If we begin to respect the voyage as much as the destination, we will be less discouraged. We will feel more confident in our ability to solve problems or discover innovations. When we base our creativity on how it stands up to the results of others, we cease to see the possibility. We begin to project the outcome and discourage ourselves from trying. We fear failure. And it's the fear of failure that causes us to fear the journey and fail.

If, for some reason, we experienced a leap in evolution and could suddenly see this journey, it would change the world as we know it. It would allow all of humanity to finally realize that every single one of us goes through these journeys. It would be yet another example of how similar we all are. It would show others why we think as we do. It would inform us as to what our motivations are and what inspires us. It would reveal a truth in how we see the world.

The value of that information is powerful and may or may not be beneficial in the long run, depending on our motivations. But the core of the idea is sound in that it asks us to accept the notion that we all take the same journey when searching for solutions.

We all act and move with the pace and tempo appropriate to what we have learned in life. Intuition tempered from our experiences, one notion leading us to the next idea. Every day we go through a chain of events within our unconscious and conscious minds that lead us to new opportunities.

For example, a need for efficiency in farming may have likely led to the invention of the plow. The plow allowed farmers to harvest far more food than they needed. This created an opportunity to sell more goods. And then suddenly an industry was born. Transporting those goods was made easier with the invention of the wheel. Suddenly there was a way to transport goods long distances at a much quicker speed. Although we don't know for a fact that the inventor of the wheel was motivated by the result of the invention of the plow, we can speculate that the invention of the wheel led to designing and development of roads. The quality of the goods that traveled on road in carts with wheels led to more efficient and effective commerce and the rest is history. Creative development and discovery is inevitable.

We will always find new ways of doing things. A deeper understanding and exploration of possibility will lead us inexorably on a journey that will change us and build our potential for growth. The question then becomes: What are we gaining from these new ideas?

12
A THEATER WITHIN A THEATER

You are not just a drop in the ocean.
You are the entire ocean in a drop.

— Rumi

A good way to consider the true power and capability of our minds is to consider something we have all done with it. Dream.

When we dream we act as the writer, director, actor, supporting actor, producer, cinematographer, cameraman, and sometimes, even stuntman. We produce this elaborate and sometimes epic story as we sleep. At the same time we watch the very story we are creating in real time. We are surprised at the very thing we create. What is it within us that we are able to act independently from conscious perception? And what effect does this detached creative element have on our creative process?

Our mind serves as a theater, where we play out our creative process. Out on the open stage we create our art of reason and intuition. We build and destroy ideas. We imagine amazing and incredible things. Within the theater of our mind lives our consciously active problem solving and deductive reasoning skills.

But behind the stage lives another smaller but very powerful inner-theater, more commonly known as the

84

unconscious mind. This inner theater's job is to gather and ignore information. We can never consider every possibility that comes in contact with our awareness.

Imagine being in a crowded cafeteria. The room is filled with noise, which we are bombarded with from every direction. Yet we can sit across from a friend and hear every word he or she is saying. Somehow, we are shielded from the noise we don't value. What is doing this? What has turned off non valuable sounds so we can focus on our areas of interest?

The part of our mind that manages our values is our unconscious. It decides what is relevant and important at any given moment. It decides what information we value and wish to retain and then offers these ideas up to our conscious mind and we decide again from this "conscious awareness" if it is relevant.

Although our conscious mind has a weakness, it's affected by fear of judgment, intimidation, shyness—all the things we struggle with and that limit us during the creative process. Our unconscious mind drives forward fearlessly and undiscouraged.

But what about free will?

Why are we limited to the whims of a portion of our mind we don't actively control? We need to realize that although we don't actively control it we do program it through learned values and inspirations. We ultimately have control over these unconscious values because we are the programmers of them. This idea is key because it suggests that our culture and environment are connected to our process of discovery. It's our conscious choices in conjunction with our unconscious programming that then gets sifted through our creative process and results in our creative output.

We can visualize the unconscious portion of our mind as a server on a network, it's job being to gather information. Our conscious mind supplies that data. The data gets stored, then delivered for us to process. That is why it's important to gather as much qualified data as possible. It gives us better material when we decide to process the information.

In a sense, our unconscious mind is programmed to react to information by our own conscious values. If we understand that by enriching ourselves through taking hard thoughtful looks at our successes and failures and by really listening and seeking out fresh data, we begin to program our unconscious mind with new ideas. We can actively begin to develop our own creative capacity and reach better solutions more quickly. If we begin to realize we are programming ourselves with impressions and values we gather throughout our day, we can then see how we are reprogramming our unconscious mind to build and deliver better, more qualified information to our conscious awareness.

13

LEADERSHIP

Queen Anne's Revenge was the name of a ship captained by the infamous pirate Blackbeard in the 1700s. We can only imagine what his colorful crew must have been like, consisting of liars, thieves, and murderers most likely suffering from a slew of undiagnosed personality disorders. He and his crew was the scourge of the Atlantic during 1717-1718. They were responsible for the capture of over 40 ships and the murder of over 4000 sailors. By pirate standards Blackbeard was very successful.

So how would a the pirate captain of one of the most dangerous and successful pirate ships in history motivate a crew consisting of a motley bunch of cut throats and criminals? Fear. It is said that he'd occasionally murder his first mate, just to keep everyone on their toes. Blackbeard knew the power of fear to motivate people and wielded it very successfully.

Fear is a viable management technique used by many organizations. You may even be able to look back in your professional career and realize that you may have also worked on a pirate ship.

Have you ever worked on a pirate ship?

Have you ever worked in a place managed by a person who felt that the only way to motivate you was to threaten you? Or even worse, fired someone just to set an example? We are judged by how we wield the powers we have. We are responsible for how we are perceived.

Blackbeard was killed November 22, 1718, yet his management style lives on today. There are basically four methods of management:

1) Extinction: The method of removing something in order to decrease a behavior we want to control. Taking something away so that an unwanted response is decreased.

2) Punishment: The method of adding something aversive in order to decrease bad or unwanted behavior. This is done so the person in question associates the unwanted act with the punishment, thus decreasing the individual's want to act again. *If I act in this unwanted manner again, the punishment will follow, therefore to avoid it, I will stop behaving in that manner.*

3) Negative Reinforcement: The action of taking something negative away in order to increase a wanted response. Like a parent continuously nagging a child about cleaning his room. When the child finally does it, to his amazement, the nagging stops. The hope is that the elimination of this nagging or negative reinforcement will motivate the child to continue cleaning his room.

4) Positive Reinforcement: The act of acknowledging people's behaviors that are beneficial or wanted. A repeated use of praise or reward in order to inform and educate people to what is the wanted response or action. This results in more positive actions and a consideration of what other actions might generate praise or reward.

Behaviors come from a collection of life experience and develop over a lifetime. People don't give change that easily. If our goal is to draw the best out of people, there has to be a want. They need to want to give us their best efforts. So if our goal is to draw out the best, the only method that will inspire this is positive reinforcement. Creating a nurturing environment is key to putting people in a giving frame of mind.

Creativity can flourish in an atmosphere where differences are welcomed and appreciated, mistakes are not mocked and ideas are fearlessly expressed. It's hard enough to deal with the self-afflicted onslaught of self-doubt and fear of failure during our own creative journey. Why impede it even more with external persecution? Our conscious mind has to manage many obstacles. Time, perception, data gathering, and strategy building require a lot of mental energy. It's intimidating to delve into the creative process if we are feeling unprepared. And although these feeling are not mutually exclusive to us, it feels as though it is because we never hear about the failures of those we model ourselves after, only their successes. We are always more effective and alert in a nurturing environment. It is important to create a safe haven where we can feel free to be who we were meant to be, free and independent. A space where our horribly misguided ideas won't be shunned or our character and reputation tarnished for a failure.

Our state of mind is a direct reflection of our environment. A happy nurturing environment creates a happy and nurturing mind that is better equipped to deal with anything it faces. But creating a comforting environment doesn't only mean we go out and buy a beanbag chair. It requires some planning. Things like making time for family and friends. Scheduling time to pursue our passions and loves. Learning something new as often as possible. Being prolific and endlessly curious. Acting on impulsive curiosities. Being engaged in life creates opportunities that become the source for new ideas. We can't create inspiration from thin air at the moment of need so it's important to gather fuel as we go that we can use to drive our creativity when we need it most.

14

A DANGEROUS IDEA

Children are fearless in the context of creative exploration. Adults… not so much.

Fear is most definitely taught and learned. Fear of taking a risk comes from the accumulation of experiences that have resulted in pain or the learned evidence of pain, regret, or shame. Fear of unforeseen consequences, or even fear of accomplishment or success keeps us from realizing our creative potential. We generally need to have good justification before we even decide to move forward with an idea or experiment.

Even though we are born with this initial courage we are constantly told as children not to touch that or stop asking questions. Or even worse: "You don't know what you are doing; let me show you." If a child is willing to try and is in no way in danger, let her try. Where is the harm? If she succeeds, it will encourage her. And if she fails, it allows us the opportunity to teach.

Fear is not an obstacle to conquer. Its purpose is to keep us safe. It warns us of possible danger and to be wary of it. Managing fear requires realizing that creativity was designed to deal with moments of fear. It's a mistake to quell the fear before going forward on an idea. Without risk there is no progress or innovative growth. Fear helps us perceive risk. Then when we conquer one fear we strive toward that next moment. It's a constant beacon calling us to push ourselves to the next point of risk. It's like a muscle that grows with regular resistance. If we fear the pain that comes from muscle resistance and stop the resistance, the muscle will stop growing and weaken. Fear is an alarm switched on by our unconscious mind protecting us from the threat of pain or suffering. It's our biggest obstacle during our creative efforts.

Our best work sits silently under the weight of our insecurity, which comes from our developmental experience. As children we were drawn to new ideas, feelings, and experiences. We actively sought them out. We needed that rush of inspiration as much as we needed the air we breathed, even if it meant putting ourselves at risk. The risk added to the gratification of the discovery.

As a parent I see how easy it is to become the spoiler of inspiration. How we protect our children from what in the grand scheme of things won't actually put them at any physical or psychological risk. We unwittingly suppress the most valuable tool in their developmental arsenal. We must remember there is rarely doom of discovery. Even if it ends badly, there is always an opportunity to grow.

We learn from a very young age that there are limitations. We are sheltered from moments that, if experienced, would teach us how to build our ability to become stronger innovators and problem solvers. We unwittingly resist creative growth. And our children carry the effects of this into adulthood.

Our natural need for an emotionally safe environment free of minimal judgment and disappointment slowly deprograms our value and need for creative nourishment. Stifling or being stifled is unfortunately inevitable. We must realize that if either of these things happens, we should act appropriately. If we are stifling someone, we'd better have a good reason to do so. We need to make sure the timing is appropriate and the person knows the reason he is being stifled. If we are being stifled, we must do our best to realize that this is not a sign that our ideas are not valuable or that our creative process is flawed. We must stay encouraged to try again.

When we are young we are primed for endless possibilities. There is a vastness to our ability to take in and process information that is quite remarkable. Consider how quickly as children we are able to learn. There are very few obstacles impeding our progress at our earliest stages of development. We have no real ego or worry of judgment. As children we live with a hunger for more knowledge and experience.

Yet people who live in parts of the world with the greatest opportunity tend to have a "give me convenience or give me death" attitude toward innovation. We resist change if it's inconvenient or difficult. It may also be because of a socially accepted fear of failure that is reinforced through our grading system that looks down on those who fail and sees them as incapable or inadequate. Maybe it's our distractions of consumerism that kills the need for creative innovation. Or a lack of motivation or understanding for how to act on inspiration.

Social media may have been the greatest tool of communication ever invented, but it also has enforced a shallowness of perception that allows us only to see things in bite-sized chunks. The immediacy in that form of communication weakens and devalues critical thinking. But we have a choice. We are not so weak minded that we need to fall into these traps. We can resist the temptation to see things from a shallow perspective.

As I sat in the lobby waiting to get some blood drawn a while back I heard a little girl screaming in terror, pleading with her mother and the phlebotomist to wait; she wasn't ready. The most heartbreaking part was hearing her mom screaming back at her daughter to shut up because she was embarrassing her. Embarrassing her how, I wondered? Her mother was afraid of the judgment of a few strangers in the lobby and staff, people who do this for a living and have likely seen scared children every day. The mother was teaching her child shame when she should have been teaching her courage.

It has often been said that our biggest obstacle to the creative process is fear of judgment from others. But it's possible that it is an actual fear of our own perception of what that judgment will be and making poor decisions because of it. We are imposing our own self-doubts on others as justification for giving up or settling on the safest idea. Fear only creates inaction or avoidance. A realization of this self-imposed perception may help us overcome our fear of failure. And even if the perceptions that cause the fear are true and the fears are proven justified, we can then begin to overcome them from a position of better understanding and more qualified skill. We learn best and most from our failures.

15
COURAGE

I was bullied a bit as a kid. I was a skinny kid then, debilitatingly shy, quiet, and a constant daydreamer. I got pushed, tripped, punched, and insulted regularly. I was called a weirdo, a dweeb, a freak... the list goes on. This was compounded by the fact that I was new to the school. I spent a great deal of my time in those days terrified of the recess bell and the inevitable physical and mental torture that would follow. The only classmate who seemed to have a more difficult time was Steven, who had the misfortune of having all of my unpopular personality traits as well as being nearsighted, a straight-A student, and the most overweight boy in school. The constant and regular torment made life very difficult at such a young age. I often fantasized about standing up to the bullies, but never had the courage.

I first witnessed an act of raw courage from an unlikely source. Steve and I were approached by a number of school bullies who wanted to include us in a game that I think was called King of the Mountain. It was a pretty simple game. Everyone stood in a circle and then counted down to zero, after which they all tried to push one another out of the circle. The last one left was the winner.

That day I had the privilege of being the first kid to hit the asphalt outside the circle. Steven, on the other hand, found a position in the center where he stood with his arms crossed, immobile and terrified, hoping nobody would notice him. The game progressed quickly. Many grunts, scrapes, tears, and bruises later, almost everyone found themselves looking in from outside the circle. Only two were left: Steven and the biggest bully.

I remember the bully, whom I think was called Calvin, had a bloodthirsty look in his eye. He circled Steven, looking him up and down as he panted, sweat dripping off his face. Circling like a shark around a wounded seal. "You're next, Steven," Calvin said. "Are you ready?" Steven steadied himself. "Here it comes!" the bully shouted as he charged with a vision war cry. We stared in amazement as we watched that horrible boy bounce off Steven's massive body and hit the ground as if he were made of rubber. Steven didn't budge – not even an inch. Everyone, including Steven, was shocked. It was then that something strange began to happen. We realized that the bully might have met his match. He continued to try to push Steven out of the circle, but still, Steven did not budge. My classmates began chanting: "Steven! Steven! Steven!" With a look of terror on his face, Steven raised his eyes up to the crowd. He noticed that the crowd had grown beyond the original group of kids involved in the game, all gathered to watch and cheer him on. The look of fear quickly switched to confusion before slowly shifting to one of confidence. Steven faced Calvin, crouched; placing one hand to the ground, and with a loud war cry, charged and knocked him out of the circle.

Calvin stood up as quickly as he could and ran away, doing his best to hide his embarrassment. Victorious, Steven the "Mountain king," the center of attention, stood taller than I'd ever seen him. And although Steven eventually went back to being the "fat kid" others picked on, he no longer cowered. He faced his tormenters, perhaps not with the dramatic flair he displayed that afternoon in the circle, but enough to where his days at school became much more bearable. I still hung out with Steven at the playground, not because I feared the bully, but because I respected Steven.

Creativity requires having the courage to put ourselves out there. Taking a chance. If we are able to take that first step we will be surprised at the outcome. We never know where inspiration will come from. And we never really know what is possible until we muster up the courage to face challenges or people who torment us.

Now, whenever I'm faced with a situation that feels impossible or intimidating, I face those fears and think of Steven. I knock the problem out of that circle because that mountain is mine.

Creative courage starts when we raise our heads and choose a target.

16
INSPIRATION

It's widely believed that inspiration cannot be forced. It's also a widely held belief that time is money. Unfortunately, these two ideas work against each other. We find that at work or school, inspiration is usually needed within a deadline. When we operate with a shallowness of perception we limit our scope of possibility. Seeing that possibility allows us to imagine and consider new avenues in the process to explore.

We can use preparation and practice to help draw inspiration in. One of the reasons creatives enjoy surrounding themselves with art, toys, trophies, sculptures, or curious trinkets is to draw ideas from them. Surrounding ourselves with reminders of our interests or successes sets up an optimistic environment to build from. We must work hard to create an environment that nurtures and inspires the creative process as much as possible. We must entertain every thought and consider every option. We can develop our creative efficiency as individuals when we realize the difference between qualified and unqualified ideas. We must leave our ego at the door and work together to find the best solution. We must allow ourselves to entertain seemingly irrelevant notions with the understanding that they can lead us to innovation and we must be fearless during the process.

Ideas are not created as much as they are captured. Opportunities constantly surround us to consider. But we tend only to see the ideas that come in a given moment. We stop the search short of possibility. It takes a while to find what we're looking for especially when we don't know what we're looking for. It seems we spend more time trying to convince ourselves our ideas are sound than finding sound ideas that need little explaining. The energy is put in the justification rather than the development. We need to trust our own qualified honest judgment as long as it's not coming from a shallowness of consideration.

A good way to develop intuition or the ability to realize when we may be on to something is to reprogram our perception. When we find ourselves liking something or inspired by something, let's take a moment to ask ourselves "why?" Finding the deeper reason of why something inspires us can be very valuable. Discovering why things capture our attention hints at our values. Ignoring is a missed opportunity. We are keeping ourselves from gathering valuable data that might help us with a current or future creative endeavor. Our perception or need to justify who we believe we are or want to be may send us on a path to avoid what we really want or need. Often people discover too late in life what they truly love to do, perhaps because later in life we are less constrained by the responsibilities of parenting or work. We are free to explore these impulses and don't fear veering off our planned agendas.

The common notion we are told in poetry or song is to always follow our heart or our gut. But that notion comes with parameters. Our gut's first priority might be to protect us, to shield us from failure. This is not the best way to explore possibility. It may discourage us into thinking we should procrastinate till we feel more comfortable. Our gut has an agenda of self-preservation that can stifle the courage necessary for innovation. We don't consider the fact that if we allow ourselves to explore possibilities, we might be rewarded with innovative ideas that make us better at the things we have to do; that we can affect the many frustrations we face with the mundane practices of life. By changing our perceptions we can rediscover these practices and have new and gratifying experiences that feed our inner needs. It may be a good exercise to experiment with breaking away from the roles we feel we need to play and find our true path in life.

There is power in sharing. It's human nature to share things that inspire us. Where some of us fall short is in stopping there. The key to becoming an innovator is sharing the results of our inspiration. Talk about what we've built because of what inspired us. Become the inspiration we are seeking. Participate in innovation. Don't just advertise it.

Thanks to our creative capacity and our ability to reason and innovate, the human organism possesses a great deal of adaptive flexibility. This is what allows us to survive in many different conditions. But we are also rigidly programed for certain environmental requirements. Just as our bodies require physical nutrients the human brain demands positive forms of environmental stimulus.

It's important to think about what kind of world we have created for ourselves. Is it helping us? Is it designed with our health—mental and otherwise—in mind? At our core, are we truly trying to be a positive source of inspiration for the people around us? Or are we going against the core values that are wired within us? That part of us that wants and works to maintain personal and social well-being?

Why do we always simply amend old solutions, thinking that will solve our current problems? We need to answer why there is a problem in the first place and why we need a solution. There has to be a fundamental shift where we all realize we are not on our own and that we ALL NEED EACH OTHER and must work to protect and support each other as we progress in life.

17
CHICKEN PICCATA

After listening to a podcast that was discussing the "Multiverse" theory, I had a dream. In this dream, I was recounting the show to my wife, Debi, who surprisingly, acted interested. Usually I get a big eye roll whenever I try to share some of these odd nerdy ideas with her. But this time was different. She actually seemed fascinated by the idea. So I took full advantage of the moment and began to explain the fascinating theory of the ever-expanding block of Swiss cheese that is the "Multiverse" theory:

How there is likely not just one universe, but multiple universes ever expanding and speeding away from each other. How this way of looking at the universe also inspires the notion that we can't possibly be alone in the universe. That we are just one of an endless number of constantly expanding universes resembling the bubbles in Swiss cheese. How the physicist on the show explained that each universe is expanding exponentially along with the space between them. That we can never reach the end of our universe in any meaningful way because it's expanding so quickly. Thus explaining why the universe seems endless to the people inside the bubble. We talked about the particles that make up the universe having a specific massive yet finite quantity, suggesting that the possibility of life beyond our universe is not only possible but also likely.

Within the dream I remember being happy. These ideas have always fascinated me and make me appreciate the complexity and beauty of life. How lucky we are to participate. How lucky I am to have a child to share these discoveries with. How meaningful it is to be able to share these moments with a woman who loves me enough to put up with me.

I remember the smell of the food she is making as we are talking. My favorite, chicken piccata. She looks up and smiles at me briefly, brushes her hair back from her face as she prepares to say something when suddenly there is a loud thud.... the wall behind her gives way along with the floor. We are in a free fall. I can see debris tumbling all around us and I'm clutching for her as she's screaming.

I have the presence of mind to realize that this is the end of everything for us. It is all coming to an end... I have run out of time. I have this oddly rational sense of panic. My thoughts go to my daughter. Is she okay? Is this happening to her? I'll never see her face again. I have to picture her in my mind before I die. I want her face to be the last image in my mind. I can feel myself kicking in the emptiness as I fall. It can't be over already. I'm not finished yet. So I call out at the top of my lungs as I reach out to my wife, my love... NO!!! .... NO!!!

At that moment my wife Debi shook me awake. My yelling "NO, NO" woke her up! Reality slowly washed over me till I became present in my safe wakened state, but I kept thinking how present I felt in the moment. How full and alive I was in one instant of the dream and then it was all taken away, so suddenly. I don't know what caused the building to collapse in my dream. All I remember is a loud thud sound, but I don't think it matters.

I do think my unconscious mind was trying to teach me something. My inner theater was warning me to wake up and pay attention. Teaching me that the moments I spend in this world are as finite as the particles in the universe? Every moment is relevant and fleeting. The sudden realization that it's coming to an end is what hit me most as I lay in my bed unable to sleep again. The desperation was powerful. I felt time passing me by. I had tasted a reality many people in our world experience outside of a dream. The smallness we feel when we consider the epic nature of the universe is palpable. But the fear of losing that seemingly insignificant life is just as epic.

My dear, Find what you love and let it kill you.
Let it drain you of your all. Let it cling onto your back and weigh you down into eventual nothingness.

— *Charles Bukowski*

React to things. Follow your intuition. Take chances. Enjoy the feeling of being surprised by the world. Being surprised is the best part of the creative process. It reminds me that life is as amazing and beautiful as it is unexplored. It's important to take a moment and enjoy it and learn from it. In the big scheme of things, life really is short. Make the most of it. Because you never know when that great dish of chicken piccata may be your last.

18

CREATIVE MATURITY

Many of us fill our lives by analyzing things around us. Things like the environment, politics, society, economics, art, parenting, crime, war, religion, etc. The list can go on forever. But one vital thing we tend to forget is to acknowledge our own ego amidst our day-to-day lives. It is our ego that motivates most of our decisions and drives us in any given direction.

We are inundated with problems daily. To succeed at any level, one must be a problem solver. One of the main obstacles in developing our ability to be that problem solver is oftentimes our inability to set our own perspective and needs aside. That's because, more often than not, many professionals have the need to be perceived as problem solvers, though that desire overrides actually being a problem solver. But there are solutions.

We must always understand that the choices we make require analytical thinking with emotional tempering. Not the other way around. Ego is a good motivator, but a terrible problem solver. Simply put, learning to manage our own ego is an effective way to process our creative exploration. Creative confidence is shown not by those creatives who say they have the best ideas, but by those who showcase their ability to be flexible, responsive, and nurturing of any good idea regardless of its origin or where that idea is headed at any given moment.

It takes a talented professional to set his ego aside and immediately listen to, discuss, address, and solve problems on the spot, all the while knowing he may not have all of the right answers just then. Addressing challenges or opportunities in this manner can be difficult for some to do, impossible for others. But, as I mentioned, this ability separates the pros from the amateurs.

Compromise requires sacrifice. Sacrifice requires humility. Humility requires confidence. Confidence comes from the development of creative maturity.

Creative maturity may seem like a contradiction in terms, but it is an absolute must when the goal is to produce the best solution possible for any situation. The dichotomy of exploring our options and ideas with a free and open mind while limiting our ego analytically isn't always easy, but it is possible.

The first step is to set aside the egotistical need to be "right" and instead learn how to trust others—and ourselves. This means allowing ourselves to be open to impromptu discussions, to step outside of our area of expertise and provide our thoughts (they do matter), to feel confident in the fact that we do have something to contribute and that our opinion is valuable.

I encourage you to put yourself and your ideas on the line, especially during those instances where there is no time to prepare. You'll be surprised at what you're already capable of doing. For the no-holds-bar always idea making, problem solving machines of the world who typically already have a highly developed sense of troubleshooting needs, I say it's okay to take a backseat at times around others who are new to this creative maturation process. Allow them to venture out, learn, and come to trust more in their own abilities and the concept that there is always more than one solution to any given problem. In doing so, it will help build their confidence.

Managing our ego is difficult to do and, as a business owner in a creative field myself, it's absolutely critical that everyone on my team is able to creatively mature. Without a proper balance of overall maturation, progress becomes more difficult. A lack of creative maturity can quickly ruin a creative culture or environment. It naturally segments itself into "control freaks" who react to pettiness and one-upmanship. A culture like this devolves into resentful groups no longer looking for solutions. Soon the team begin to create their own self-imposed walls that hinder their own progress and growth. Arguments become clouded in a fog of agenda and value justification.

An efficient and effective way to reach the best solution in the shortest amount of time is to commit to muting our emotional needs to be right. And to realize that a sacrifice of need is often required for the best solution.

But this goes both ways. If we find ourselves in a position where we've been shown respect and gratitude for our idea, we need to remember to return the favor. This builds strong creative collaboration which in turn builds a strong creative culture that will act as a virtual idea machine that fuels itself.

Creative Courage *with Alex Raffi*

19
SHUT UP AND WORK

We all get frustrated. We feel impatient. We feel discouraged. We try to shift the pieces so they make sense. The belief that the world is a puzzle for us to decode is daunting, demotivating, and inaccurate. Just shut up and work. All that noise feels like progress but in actuality becomes wasted energy. The bottom line is we need to do what we are good at. And do it a lot. Never stop. Not get too hung up on the results of the work because the act of working consistently with commitment yields progressively improving results. The act of work creates opportunities and is the birthplace of innovation. Trust that putting our energy into something will lead us to where we need to go.

Shut up and work. Stop trying to second-guess our progress. Stop talking ourselves out of taking chances. Stop placing judgment on the validity or value of our work. Stop fighting the richness of our capacity. Shut up and work. If we're good at what we do, we'll get better. If we're great at what we do it will show. We must do what we are good at. And do it a lot. Never stop. Shut up and work. Nothing will fall in our lap. We need to keep our eyes open for opportunities and act on them. Nobody owes us any favors. It's up to us to shut up and work.

It's important to keep active and always search for new ideas to express and study. Our creative ability isn't always as reliable as we would hope. We can't always be functioning at full capacity so it's important to stay active. Much like with our physical health, our creative health requires constant exercise and nutrition. It must be kept fueled with fresh ideas and challenges. Although the consumption of the creative endeavors of others is gratifying, it's possible we are misinterpreting inspiration for gratitude. Taking those positive feelings and channeling them into our work or relationships will develop a richer environment that will yield more inspiration as we go forward.

20
WHAT TO AVOID

Our creative switch is always on the on position. It's not a conscious act. We are often not even aware it is happening. If we aren't consciously aware we are using our creative tools, then it's likely we are also not aware that we are obstructing its process. Most of the time it's not intentional. We dampen it by replacing our best creative processes with emotional need, doubt, fear, anger, or pure laziness, to name a few.

The list of things that keep us from exploring our creative potential are endless. Identifying them and acknowledging that they are obstacles is a good start to avoiding them. It requires self awareness and discipline to go against our natural inclination.

The inner critic is a big one. It will always be our greatest enemy. It comes from our fear of being judged or of being perceived as talentless or ignorant. This is a difficult hurdle to overcome, but it is the most important one because our best work will always be left at the bottom of a pile of self doubt.

Piling on messages is another one we don't think of. This happens often, especially with people who don't understand the creative process. People try to cram as much as possible into one idea, but there is a limit to the weight an idea can bear. A cluttered, complex idea may feel gratifying to the creator, but it will only be an obnoxious mess to the observer. The message must be precise and to the point. It is important to realize that although there is no limit to the process one goes through to come up with an idea, there is a limit to effective creativity in the end product.

Lack of knowledge on a topic is not always realized. To ensure the most effective outcome, it makes sense to be as informed as possible. If you have been hired to create something for a client, you really need to understand everything about the topic at hand. Understand or at least try your best to know as much as possible that is relevant to the goal. After a while, you will find that going through this procedure will become natural in your problem-solving process. Again, being aware of the possibility of error from lack of data will become a red flag during your process. Trust that feeling and act accordingly by doing research. And remember to ask questions. Your intuition will guide you on what to ask.

I often find myself asking questions that may not seem relevant to anyone but myself. I believe temporarily pulling people away from the topic at hand ensures that they will answer the question without editing it according to their perceived notion of what I want to hear. From that answer I can then deduce a new direction that might help me find a solution.

There needs to be an objective as well as a limit to the development of ideas. If a person offers an idea nobody likes, she should be given a chance to explain why the idea can be effective. It is unwise to kill ideas immediately. Great ideas have often come from concepts that were initially disregarded but fought for. That being said, if the idea is still not effective to the majority after it's explained, move on.

It's odd to think that it is often possible to be "too creative." There is a tendency to get excited about an idea and take it way too far. Getting caught up in the excitement feels good. We may find ourselves wanting to ride that wave a bit farther than necessary. The risk is a lack of clarity. Exploring concepts is dandy, but there is a fine line between creative exploration and wasting time. Always remember the objective and realistic implementation of an idea. It's a balancing act that may feel contradictory, but we need to remember to stay on time and within budget. Trust our creative judgment while avoiding our fear of failure. Nobody ever said it would be easy.

21
MOMENTS OF DISCOVERY

Life is full of challenges. We require a reason to face them head on. If we have a pulse, we have a purpose. But do we know what that purpose is? One way to figure it out is to look back into our life history and relive the time we made the decision to be who we are. We all need to identify our moment or moments of discovery, the moments when something profound happened to us in our life. The moment that we came face to face with an idea that has stuck with us and defined our purpose in life.

We each have our own way that we look at life. We each have a unique perspective. A perspective that influences how we see the world around us. There is at the very least one moment in everybody's life that helps define who we are. Looking back at those moments is important because they remind us of who we are and why we are driven to do what we do.

Do you know yours?

Once it's identified, you can begin to draw inspiration from the moment. Whether it's a good moment or bad, you must keep it close. Awareness of who you are is key to becoming a better problem solver.

Everyone has an influence on the world. No matter how small we may think it is, it's still an influence. If we all realized the influence we as individuals had on the world, we would be ready to meet any challenge that comes before us with more courage and creativity. We would strive forward armed with self awareness and confidence in our capacity to cope with anything that came our way.

Every organized action—be it a business, project, or movement—begins with a vision. Someone somewhere had an idea that was meant to fill a void.

From our discoveries comes our dream for a way we want our lives to be. From that dream comes the vision of what it will be. From that vision comes a purpose. There is power in that purpose. The power necessary to do great things.

Things aren't always that easy, though. We do fail. In those times we have to shift our focus and "wise up." Because failure is not the enemy. Failure is the teacher. It teaches us our boundaries. In our times of failure, we must find the ability to create our own opportunities. We may need to focus on developing new relationships or begin to nurture our old ones. Things feel like they are in flux during those times but one thing has not changed: that thing that drove us in the early days. That moment of discovery.

My parents have always been very supportive of me. As a boy I lived in Orange County where my father owned a frame shop. I would go there to help out. I really loved having access to all the wood scraps, paint, canvas, and gesso. I quickly learned that I had everything I needed to build and stretch my own canvases. This allowed me to work and explore my creativity in a way that truly helped define who I am. It was the inspirer of many moments of discovery for me. Here is one that I will never forget.

Every year the city of Costa Mesa held a "Fish Fry" where, for a fee, locals could rent booths and hock their wares. My father offered to pay for a space to show some of my paintings. One of the pieces I was sharing that day had been inspired by a Marlboro ad I had seen. But instead of depicting the cigarette-smoking cowboy, I had replaced him with a nondescript and rough sketch of a Native American riding a horse at full gallop through the desert at sundown.

As the day progressed, people stopped by and shared their questions about my inspiration and technique. Some were very polite, others not so much. Toward the end of the day a man visited me who had stepped away from his booth to take a look around. I had seen him earlier on my way to grab some fish and chips for lunch. He was manning the POW booth at the end of my row. He looked hard. He looked like a man who had seen quite a bit in his life. Today he chose to spend some time looking at my painting of the Native American. He stared long enough that I started feeling uncomfortable. I wondered what he was looking at. Did he like it? Did he hate it? I had no idea, though I remember feeling intimidated.

I noticed all his medals. One stood out to me. Even at that young age I understood what a man had to go through to earn a purple heart. He turned to me, pointed at my painting of the Native American and asked if I'd painted it. I nodded and was surprised at the look on his face. With tears in his eyes, he told me one of his moments of discovery, of how terrified he was the first time he landed in enemy territory in Vietnam. He described how it felt being in the jungle for the first time. He described the moment he met up with a company of seasoned soldiers on the ground. He described one man in particular, who was unusually kind to him. This stranger took this frightened young man under his wing. He began to teach him. He taught him how to survive in that jungle. He shared ideas and stories from his Native American culture. He taught him how to look out for things that were not interested in being found. He rattled off many lessons I didn't understand but could feel were very important. But the most important lesson was the last one he mentioned. He taught him what it meant to be a man. The person he described was a father figure to him.

Then he paused and told me that this incredibly important man died in that jungle. A man who helped define how he sees the world now. He described the guilt he felt that he had not allowed himself to think of this man in all these years. Not until the moment he looked at my painting. For some reason this painting pulled those emotions out of him.

As a fifteen-year-old, I knew nothing about life—let alone death and war. I was confused by most of what had just happened in front of me. I wrote it off as a story to share with friends. It wasn't till I became older and reflected back on it that I identified it as a very important moment of discovery for me.

Creative Courage *with Alex Raffi*

How could a painting I created stir something so powerful in a man who had endured emotions I couldn't imagine? It didn't make sense. Where did that come from?

I then realized that creativity is not just about art. It is more than just a tool to communicate and touch people at an emotional level. The value of creativity is not in the result of the action; it is the actual action that is important. I knew I wanted to continue searching for those moments. This was my moment of discovery. A moment that taught me we can not predict the effect our creative process will have. The process needs to happen without expectation or prediction.

Now when I'm faced with the worry that I will not find a solution, I think about that moment of discovery and realize I don't need to define my outcome. I need to let the process discover it and trust that my own intuition will guide me.

22
IDEAS

Creative Courage *with Alex Raffi*

Most of the world is covered by water. A fisherman's job is
simple: Pick out the best parts.
— Charles Waterman

Ideas are the result of a convergence of many experiences,
large and small. These experiences are like "tokens" we
gather and bring together as ingredients that result in a
solution or idea. These tokens inspire us. The feeling of
inspiration is a signal. In much the same way that pain is a
signal for danger, inspiration is the signal for opportunity.
It acts as a kind of beacon drawing our attention to an
opportunity.

Yet we also feel pressure to pull these tokens from thin air.
That is a big obstacle to overcome. We find ourselves
struggling with this during our creative endeavor. We need
to realize that we are not the creator of these tokens and for
the most part we don't need to go looking for them. They
will likely come to us. We automatically trigger the process
when we decide we need a solution. Our unconscious mind
feeds our mental search. It's up to us to capture these
tokens as they come.

We must try not to ignore our impulse to place judgment on
the value of a token and remember it isn't a complete idea
yet. It's likely part of an idea that will meld or collaborate

with another that will then become the idea. We really have no way of seeing into the future and realizing the whole until we go through the process.

But where do we get those ideas? Remember, ideas are captured; they don't just fall into our lap. We need to pay attention to what comes to mind. In essence, we are hunters in search for the right kind of tracks in the form of inspiration.

Where will we hunt? Are we in a place that will allow us to find that inspiration? What form of trap will we set and what kind of bait will we use? Are we primed and willing to explore our inspiration regardless of our preconceptions of their true value?

These idea tokens come in many shapes and sizes. They come and go randomly—and without warning—they disappear. It's our job to catch these tokens in whatever way possible. It's important to realize that many opportunities to catch these ideas are being missed. We need to hone our ability to notice and attract the best ones. We can improve our chances by paying attention to how we attract them and repeat that process. If we are open and welcoming, they will come. Then we capture those ideas, prepare them, and deliver them. Remember, ideas are not created; they are captured. Creativity is in the preparation of those ideas. If we stay alert and react when we notice opportunities, we will be able to feed our creative needs endlessly and efficiently.

23
OPPORTUNITIES

I was on my computer scrolling through friends' social media posts one day and paused; one curious post looked like a home video. A friend shared a cute animated gif of a little boy standing in front of a Superhero piñata, holding a decorated stick. There was no sound but I could see he was being coaxed into knocking the candy out of the Superhero piñata. But instead of cracking it open, he was only lightly tapping it with the stick. Finally realizing his heart wasn't into it, the adult near him took the stick from him. As soon as the stick left his fingers, he walked up to the Superhero piñata and gave at a loving hug. I could see his deep regret and shame in that hug.

How many times have we made assumptions on people's reactions based on acceptable norms rather than considering the needs and perceptions of the target audience? Nobody took a moment to consider how this boy felt about the Superhero or how he would feel about what he was being asked to do. He was placed into an accepted system designed to build excitement at the party and create a memory, a photo opportunity of two dozen kids scrambling for candy pouring out of a cardboard Superhero. The thought of this boy's reaction wasn't even a priority, yet it affected the outcome.

Don't get me wrong. Proven systems are relevant, especially if we've had positive results from them. But what are our limitations, if any? Have we identified all of our opportunities? What are the projected consequences? Are we making an educated guess during the implementation portion of our creative process?

Creativity doesn't only have one speed. I've developed an "Idea Arc" that illustrates a method of going through the creative process with eight important steps to consider.

(1) The problem. Make sure we have a good grasp of what it is we want to accomplish. Not what the solution is. What need does it fill? Starting from a blank canvas is never the best jumping off point. In fact, there is no such thing as a "blank canvas," because we possess an entire life of experiences that will help guide us. We can start a creative endeavor with a goal of coming up with a new chicken recipe by discussing or describing a vacation we took the previous year. In other words, we just start working. Eventually we will find the hook that will catch on to our goal of developing a new dish. We must trust that our creative process will come through.

(2) Establishing freedom: We must create a safe environment that fosters and welcomes innovation and encourages rather than stifles. This is important in a group but also must be considered when we are alone. We stifle ourselves more than we realize.

(3) Exploration: The journey is key to everything. This is the moment when we consider our goals and objectives. The moment when we identify opportunities and evaluate their value. This is where we must spend the majority of our time and linger even after we think we have finished. Be free in it. It's when we are expected to make discoveries. Live in the exploration.

(4) Creative Reaching: This is the moment that scares us the most, when we allow ourselves to get off topic. From other people's perspective, it's when we seem distracted from the bigger goal. 'Avoid shiny things and stay focused' is the typical motto here. What we don't realize is that sometimes we're taken off track for a reason. Sometimes the exploration opens up opportunities that aren't initially identifiable. Greatness happens in these moments if we pay attention and stay curious as to why we are being distracted. But always remember that we eventually need to bring it back and focus.

(5) Focus. Our goal is to come to a conclusion, so at some point we need to kick in our left hemisphere and focus our work in some coherent way.

(6) Creative Reach (again) ... optional. I like to throw in a little creative reach exploration again to test the waters. It helps validate the work and strengthens the resolve of the solution.

(7) Compromise. We need to compromise sometimes, to figure out if we are solving a problem or satisfying a feeling. Try to be practical and self-aware. Is there a grander perception of the process that is being ignored because of ego or personal irrelevant needs?

(8) The Solution. Execution and implementation is crucial. We have just gone through an amazing process that must be expressed and shared. Find the best way to do this and follow through.

24
THE CREATIVE ARC

The creative arc is a visual example of an effective brainstorm session. The arc was created to help us through the process and embrace the unpredictability of creativity.

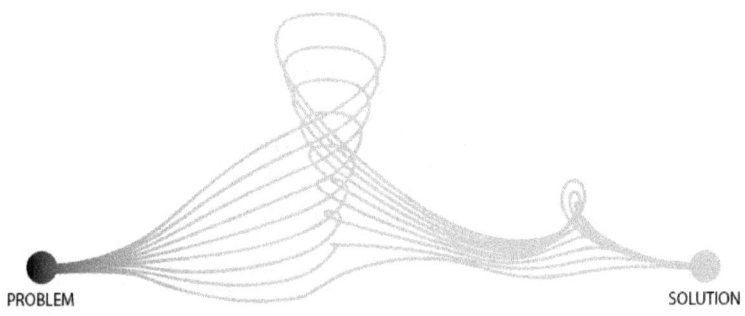

The path from problem to solution is never linear, but it's important to understand the order of events. If we understand the process then we can be unafraid to explore seemingly unimportant, or seemingly irrelevant, ideas.

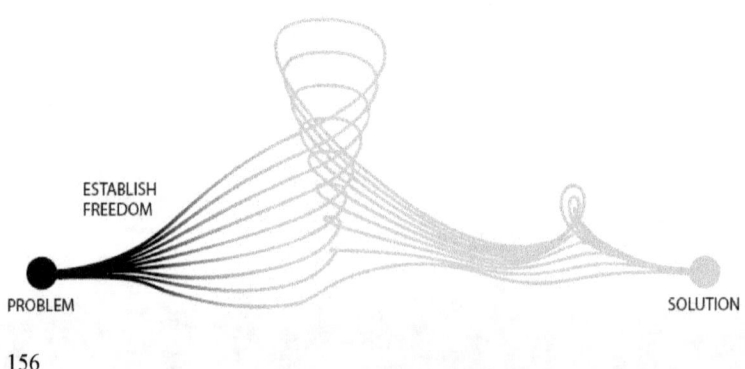

Establish Freedom:

At the beginning it is important that everyone feels free to share ideas without judgment. The problem lies when people self edit. We don't have the advantage of exploring the seeds of possibility if they are never revealed. We don't need to have a complete idea before we share it. We must create an environment that encourages exploration by removing all negativity that may stifle fledgling ideas.

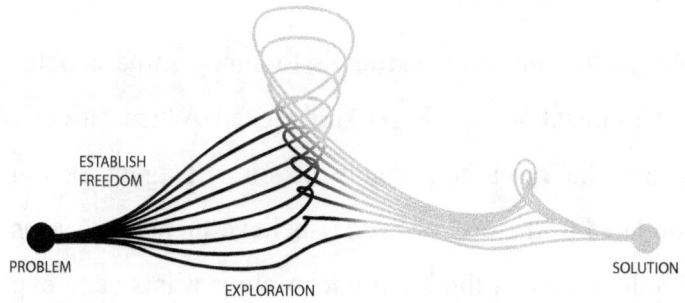

Exploration:

This is when we jump into analyzing possibilities. We ask many questions and consider many solutions. We share and listen and leave nothing off the table. Exploration means just that. Let's truly explore possibilities in a safe environment. Be as broad as we can be at this stage.

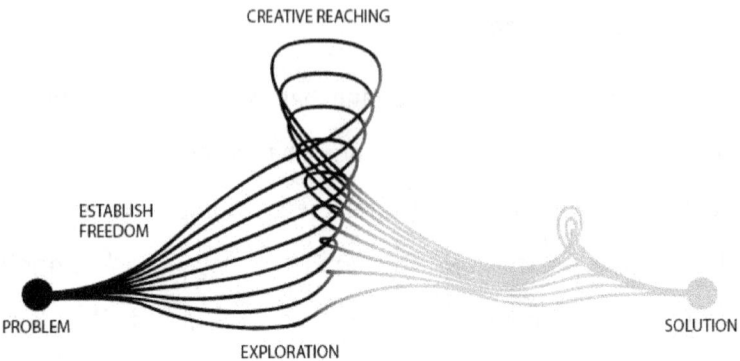

CREATIVE REACHING

ESTABLISH
FREEDOM

PROBLEM

SOLUTION

EXPLORATION

Creative Reaching:

This is that moment that tends to annoy some people. It's that moment when we get sidetracked. When an occasion within the discussion sends us on a tangent seemingly unrelated to the task at hand. I believe there is a reason for this distraction. I think our unconscious wants us to explore an idea from a new perspective. We must not be afraid of the distraction. Have the courage to explore it a bit. I hope we realize we are disciplined enough to do so and then circle back on track. Many of my or my colleagues' best ideas have come from these unexpected tangents.

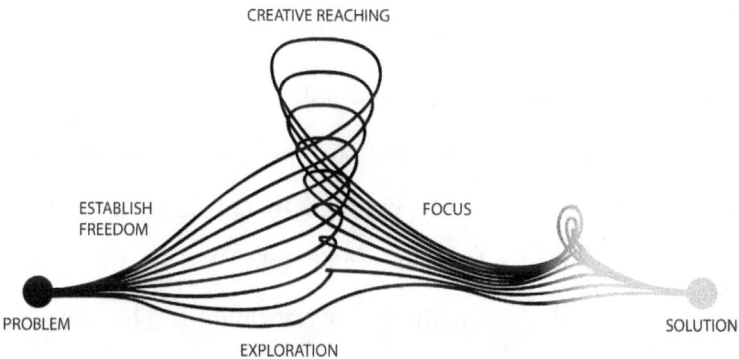

Focus:

At the end of the day the object is to come up with a solution, which requires coming to a conclusion. There must be a point in every creative endeavor that we consider the end of the search. Then we must begin to focus the results of our exploration and manifest the semblance of a solution.

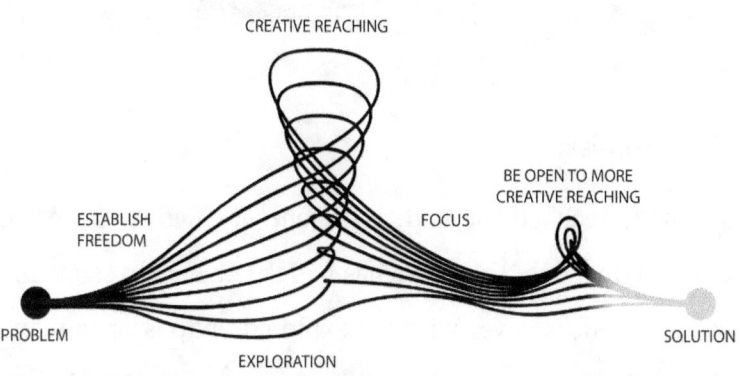

Be open to second creative reach:

I wouldn't consider doing this unless there is time and an open mind to allow ourselves to be distracted. I've found that we always have the courage to consider new ideas. This process is fluid and unpredictable. We are in essence trying to control something uncontrollable. The creative process has a life of its own and our conscious mind needs to follow its lead. The better we become in trusting our creative process the easier this will be.

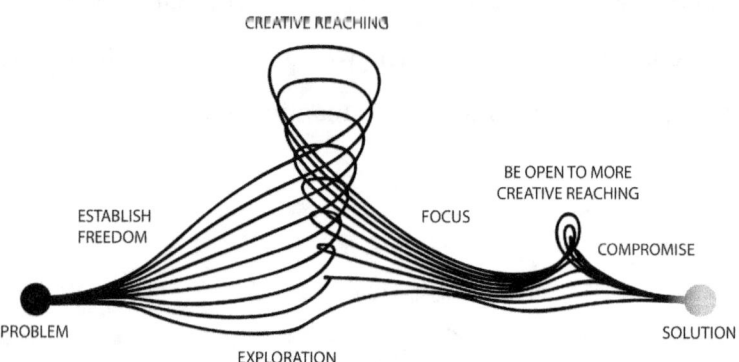

Compromise:

We have reached the end. Everyone has had a chance to offer alternatives. Everyone has had the chance to share and challenge ideas. Everyone has explored options openly and shared their considerations of the outcome of the solution.

We are at the end of our process. It's time for everyone to get onboard and make this idea shine.

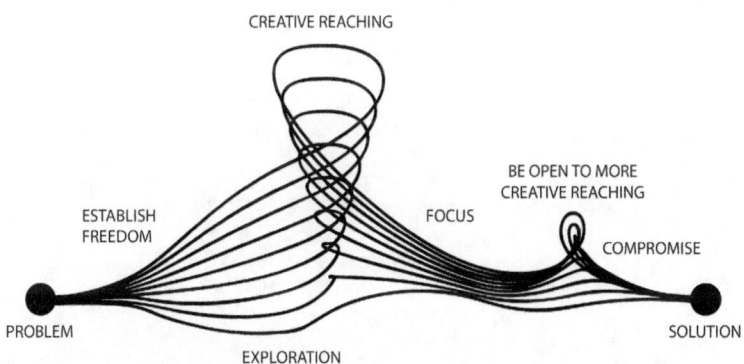

Implementation:

We have a solution to implement. Now everyone must know their role in its implementation. No one leaves before understanding their part in the solution. This step is often forgotten in creative meetings. A good solution poorly implemented is a waste of our efforts. We must be sure to have a strong implementation strategy.

25
EGO

Creative Courage requires turning off our ego while we are earning the right to have one.

Sigmund Freud describes the ego as our inner influence that represents what we call reason and sanity; in contrast, he identifies the id as the source of our passions. Reason and sanity protect us from harm. They keep us safe from all seen and perceived dangers in the world. But our reason and sanity, although valuable, can stifle our creative process.

Leading with passion is key to manifesting possibility. Passion unlocks the optimism needed to trust our ability to find answers. Remember, our ego has been crafted from failures as well as successes. It's a learned device. Freeing ourselves of the predictable encourages grander visions and creates more possibilities.

The most common description of our ego is a person's sense of self-esteem or self-importance. These are not bad attributes but can create blind spots if we don't also consider self-awareness. Honest self-awareness keeps our perspective clear. It's important to trust our own judgment but not without tempering it with an honest consideration of what is truly motivating our actions.

A few years back I was scheduled for a root canal. I did my best to prepare myself for some intense oral surgery. I scanned the room around me attempting to predict what was about to happen. I looked at all the equipment and tried to imagine it being awkwardly forced into my mouth. I was definitely feeling a bit of anxiety.

The doctor finally came in and reassured me it was going to be fine. His words put my mind at ease. I lay back, opened my mouth, and relaxed. Everything was going smoothly. During each step of the operation, the doctor informed me as to what to expect. I got used to the high pitch squeal of the drill and my mind wandered a bit.

He kept squirting blue liquid into the hole in my tooth between drilling. I think he said, "This will kill the nerves in your tooth. It's pretty much bleach!"

I responded with thumbs up.

Unfortunately, about a quarter of the way into the process the syringe cracked and the bright blue nerve-killing liquid poured directly into my nasal cavity and left eye. At first I felt a sharp sting coupled with a drowning sensation as I swallowed some of the bleach-like liquid. Then I felt a slow burning. As I rose to my feet in pain, the doctor gasped and immediately walked me over to the sink so I could rinse my eyes.

"Are you okay?" he kept asking me.

I took a mental inventory of my situation and answered honestly, "I'm fine." For some strange reason I made a choice at that moment to consider the situation as a whole. I was overcome with the idea that I needed to make the doctor feel at ease, realizing this was not done on purpose.

After thirty minutes of rinsing and gargling, I returned to my dental chair, all the while assuring the doctor that I was not angry and that I understood it was equipment failure and a rare occurrence.

I took notice of the doctor: his excellent bedside manner and empathy; his manner during the process before the syringe broke and after; and the fact that it clearly wasn't intentional or avoidable. He even went to the extent of calling my Lasik surgeon to make certain my eye would be okay. Everything in me was telling me to get really angry but I chose to go against my gut reaction and actively fought my emotional need to express anger.

The result was positive. I was able to sit through the rest of my surgery.

At these moments our innovation and adaptive skill really kick in. I was in full control of how this experience would go. I held all the cards. This is always an option. Instead of leading the outcome of a process I chose to ride it out. We gather energy from any given experience and inject that energy into our reaction whether it is anger, sadness, inspiration, or creative action. It's our choice to own the moment and respond in a way that best suits our situation. But if our reactions are always the same and predictable, we will never know our true capacity.

Because of my reaction, I'm sure the doctor's response was affected. We don't interact with each other through a bubble. Our reactions—our verbal and physical communications—fuel the verbal and physical reactions of others. I learned a bit about myself from that interaction. And I'd guess the doctor did the same.

On that very same day, on my way home, traffic was terrible. Cars were honking all around me. People leaned out their windows trying to catch a glimpse of the idiot holding up everything. As I got closer I noticed it was an automobile accident. The damage to both vehicles seemed to be significant. A man stumbled around his small car and went into the back seat to reveal a baby carrier. Hands bloodied, he pulled the baby out of the vehicle and lurched toward the sidewalk.

I pulled my car over to the side of the road and called 9-1-1 as I ran toward him. The man was clearly in shock and appeared to be injured. A few other people pulled over as well to check on the vehicle blocking traffic in the other direction. I heard honking in the distance from other cars that have not made their way close enough to see what had happened.

The dispatcher on the other end of my phone had me give her a synopsis of the situation. I bent down to check the baby who was strapped tightly into his car seat and seemed fine. After giving all the information I walked into a nearby convenience store and bought some water, which I handed out to all the accident victims sitting very dazed in the 110-degree heat. Once the firemen arrived I got into my car and left.

That day there were many ways people could have reacted to the situation. Some with impatience, not because they were cold-hearted or lacked empathy for the accident victims. They were annoyed because they made an immediate and incorrect assumption about the reason for the inconvenience. They responded with pessimism rather then curiosity. But it was impossible at that moment to realize or know why it happened.

We tend to guess the outcome of situations with gut reactions all the time. We make assumptions that lead us into impatient, unqualified reactions and decisions. Decisions that will affect our problem-solving process. This is probably the most common way we fuel our choices. It takes a strong will to work against these initial feelings, but we may be surprised at what we find.

The idea that we have enough information to make blanket predictions on a given situation often lead to poor, unqualified solutions. We need to ride out the process and not be so confident that our predictions and judgments are always true. Better clues to the truth will be revealed to us if we take the time to slow down and discover them. Understanding our own creative capacity requires an exploration of what will happen when we go against our gut. Going against these impulsive feelings will reveal things about ourselves. It will build confidence and in turn build our ego. An honest and strong ego will allow us to broaden our perspective, allowing in more possibilities and better choices.

26
NUANCE

Creative Courage *with Alex Raffi*

What was said to the rose that made it open
was said to me here in my chest.

— Jalaluddin Rumi

Nuance surprises us. It is illusive. There is eloquence in the practice of a well-implemented skill set that takes us to a higher experience. We often don't seek it out. It just sneaks up and takes its place beside us as we explore possibilities during our creative journey. It quietly breathes life into our work that elevates it beyond expectations. Even the implementer is surprised at the beauty of fluency in the act. It is the unexpected insertion of life into the adequate expression of a thing. We don't consciously do anything different to activate the effects of nuance. It reveals itself in the results.

We hear this very clearly in music. An amateur cellist can take a sheet of music and play every note perfectly. Not one technical error. Not one missed beat. Yet the same sheet of music in the hands of a seasoned cellist results in something very different. The same notes are played in the same order and tempo, yet there is a life within the melody not gotten from the amateur. There is fullness to the execution that only comes from complete faith in intuition and skill.

This is also true in our creativity. The creative process is a skill to be mastered. We begin to focus less on the acquisition of ideas and innovations and begin to act instinctively and trust our judgment. We trust it so deeply that we are able to live in the process.

In the same way we become familiar with a musical instrument. Our understanding and implementation of creativity at its fullest capacity becomes a common practice. We then become less focused on our technique and more focused on the experience of expression. We live it rather than execute it. It becomes synonymous with our expression rather than what we do to express ourselves. It is the moment all creatives chase. That moment when everything comes together as they were always meant to. A sculptor sees the sculpture within the granite and simply removes the pieces that were not meant to be there. It's the moment when we are finally creatively free.

27
CHANGING THE ROOM

I took an experimental art class in college where each of us spent time building a piece of art in pretty much any format we wanted. Then we each took turns presenting it to the class and accepting criticism of the work. It taught us how to realize our strengths and build up a thick skin to deal with judgment. Although we each worked in many different mediums—sculpture, photography, paint—we all respected the process and the energy generated from it. I learned something from everyone in that class.

On one particular occasion my painting consisted of a kind of deep-sea zombie tapestry. I carved out a piece of wood, then mounted a canvas to it. I then painted a figure over the piece and weighed it down at the bottom with another piece of wood. The figure was up to his jaw in what looked like raw sewage. He seemed to be flailing about in it, struggling with a lifeless look on his face. No expression really. The painting hung nine feet from the tallest portion of the classroom. I called it, "The drowning man."

I proceeded to describe my motivations that in those days, like most of my work, had to do more with exploring medium than exploring any kind of deep meaning or artistic expression. Most of the questions were about technique and color choice. Others used words like "disturbing" and were curious about my emotional state. I always had a hard time explaining my inspiration or

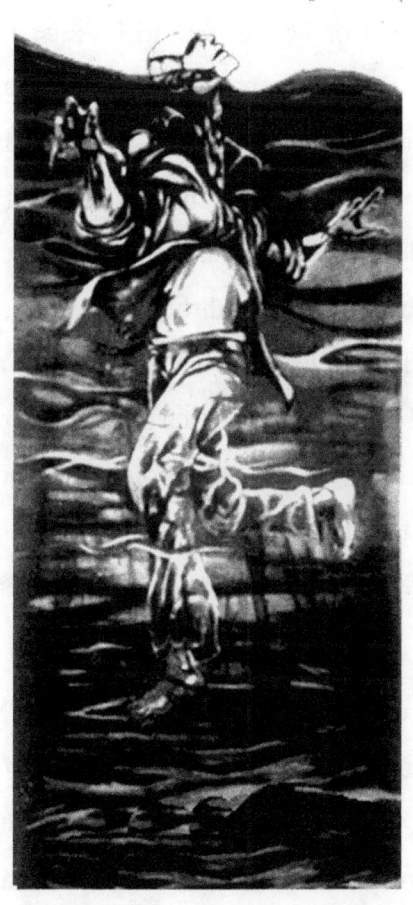

motivation for the meaning I was trying to convey. I had to admit that I just wanted to build a tapestry with a carved piece of wood at the top. The idea of painting the figure came after to accommodate the head shape I had created.

My recollection of that afternoon was that there was a unanimous indifference for the painting and my lackluster presentation. I felt a bit dejected and embarrassed. Once everyone had his or her chance to critique my work our teacher, Tom Dowling, stood up. He took a moment to observe the painting and then addressed the class. He began to explain how he believed this was a very optimistic painting. He described the thickness of the muck the man in the painting had to trudge through. He talked about the fighting and clawing he must have done to be able to make his way to the top. Treading water, fighting for his life. Yet the moment captured was victorious. He reached the top and was able to take in a breath. He fought his way to the top, yet we all placed judgment on his success from below the water line.

Suddenly there was a shift in our awareness. Mr. Dowling offered opened our eyes to a new perception of the painting we didn't realize. And we all liked this new perception and began to own it. Everyone in the room, including me, began to see their work in a more thoughtful way. There was now deeper value in the context of my work. Mr. Dowling did something very difficult that day. He changed the room. He taught us to see past our shallow perceptions and identify another possibility.

It's a wonderful thing to witness that moment. When we are able to externally make that shift of understanding that usually occurs internally so that everyone can experience it. Finding an idea unique enough to move others to want to be part of it only comes from an exceptional ability to be open to possibility.

So the next time we decide to pass judgment on an idea, let's ask ourselves if we've allowed our perspective to rise high enough. It's up to us to decide when we are going to stop looking. It's up to all of us to make a choice to either settle or claw our way up through the muck of self doubt or short-sighted judgments and accept our reward of clarity at the top.

28
LET'S DRAW

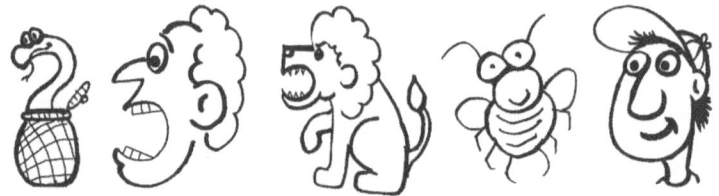

Sometimes kids, as well as adults, have a hard time knowing how to start a drawing. The process we go through in developing a simple drawing is a great way to exercise our perceptive muscles. And it can even be fun. This method of using a number to get started always seems to inspire kids who think they can't draw and helps unlock some courage in their exploration of creative capacity. The interesting thing is that it also helps us adults see that sometimes the secret to discovering our capacity comes from approaching a problem from a completely different perception.

Here are some examples of how to dig deep and see possibility in places you wouldn't expect. Once you try drawing the images shown here, try coming up with your own and also try using other numbers or letters.

Draw a snake in a basket from a number 2.

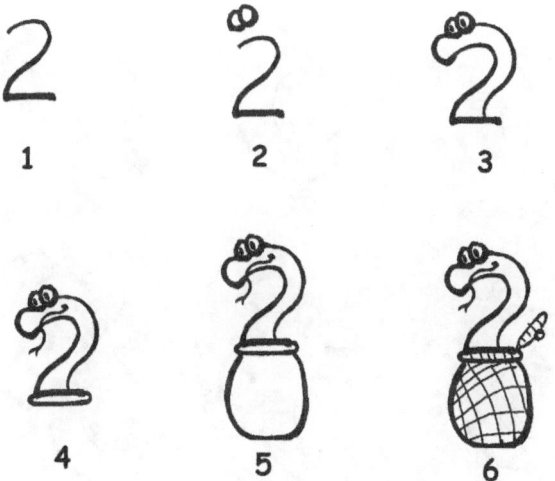

Draw a person yelling from a number 3.

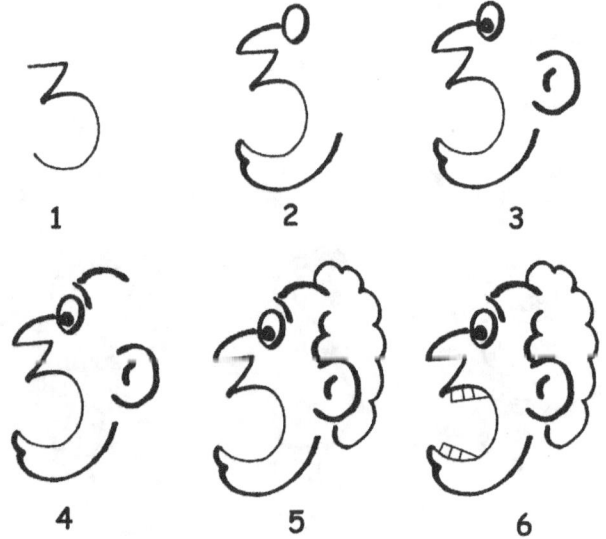

1

2

3

4

5

6

Draw a lion from a number 5.

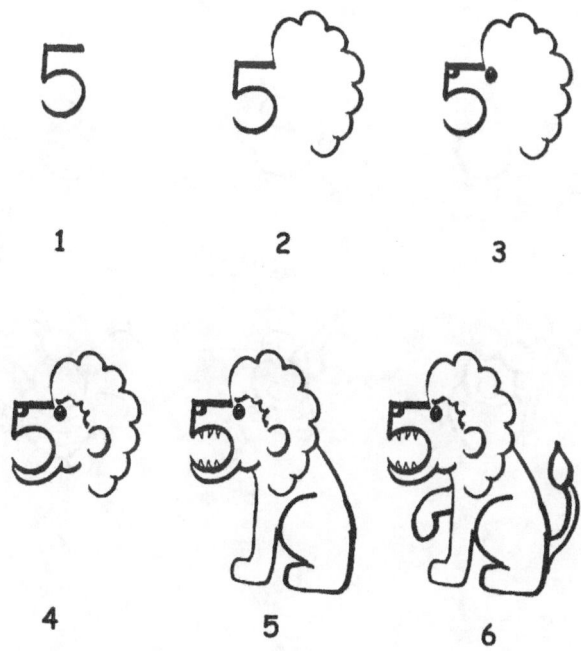

Draw a house fly from a number 8.

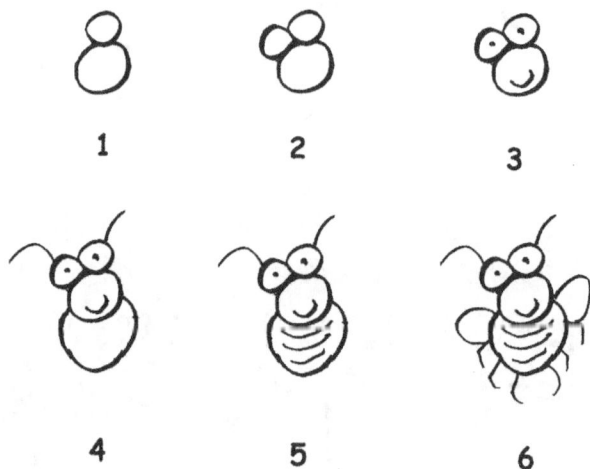

Draw a face from a number 9.

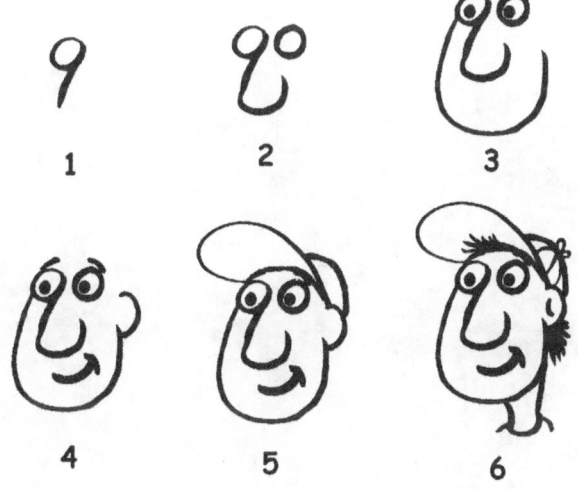

ABOUT THE AUTHOR

Alex Raffi is a husband, father, business owner, creative director, author, and illustrator. He has worked as an editorial cartoonist, animator, and caricature artist.

A multiple first-place winner with the Nevada Press Association for his illustrations, Alex joined Imagine Marketing in 2001. Since that time the firm has expanded to fifteen employees and is one of the fastest-growing firms of its kind in the market. As partner and creative director, now called Imagine Communications, Alex and the design team have created and assisted in the development of branding materials for numerous organizations throughout Nevada.

A true advocate for creativity, Alex has made it his goal to demystify the creative process with as many people as possible through his highly acclaimed Creative Courage program. He is a sought-after guest speaker who has conducted workshops and seminars for a variety of organizations and schools throughout Southern Nevada, including: The Charter School Association of Nevada, Zappos.com, The Henderson Chamber of Commerce, SMPS Las Vegas, The American Institute of Architects Las Vegas, The American Marketing Association of Nevada, University of Nevada Las Vegas, Nevada State College, Clark County School District, Orange Coast College, and the LABMAN2014 event. A longtime Nevadan, Alex is actively involved in the community. He is on the Henderson Chamber of Commerce Foundations Board. He has served as a big brother for the Big Brothers, Big Sisters program and is a mentor and presenter for the Children of the Arts program. He is also on the committee for the Narrative Illustration Program at Orange Coast College. In 2016, Alex received the **Nobel Award** at the Henderson's 16th Annual Economic Development & Small Business Awards in recognition of how much he has given back to the business community.

Additionally, since 2007, Alex has been a proud supporter of St. Baldrick's, a volunteer-driven charity committed to funding the most promising research to find cures for childhood cancers and giving survivors long and healthy lives.

You can learn more at www.alexraffi.com and at Alex's Creative Courage blog site, www.yourcreativecourage.com.

www.ingramcontent.com/pod-product-compliance
Lightning Source LLC
Chambersburg PA
CBHW072136170526
45158CB00004BA/1399